PASSIVE INCOME ONLINE

2 BOOKS IN 1:
DROPSHIPPING, MAKE MONEY ONLINE WITH DROPSHIPPING

Table of Contents

DROPSHIPPING

Description 7
Introduction.. 9
Chapter 1 The Advantages of Working in Drop shipping... 16
Chapter 2 Getting Ideas on What Products to Choose....... 24
Chapter 3 Finding the right niche 36
Chapter 4 Find and Work with the Right Suppliers 49
Chapter 5 Building the website 58
Chapter 6 How to Run Your Drop Shipping Company...... 68
Chapter 7 The Dropshipping Model of Business 81
Chapter 8 Shopify Dropshipping 84
Chapter 9 How to Dropship on Amazon and eBay 96
Chapter 10 What to do next?... 98
Chapter 11 Taking a Look at Current Trends 101
Chapter 12 Social Media Approach in Dropshipping........ 113
Conclusion 119

MAKE MONEY ONLINE WITH DROPSHIPPING

Description 123
Introduction 125
Chapter 1 Understanding Dropshipping 127
Chapter 2 Why Invest in Dropshipping? 130
Chapter 3 What You Need for a Successful Dropshipping Business 139
Chapter 4 Three ways to run a functional dropshipping store 149
Chapter 5 How Much Money Will I Need to Start My Business? 158
Chapter 6 Setting Up Your Dropshipping Business 174
Chapter 7 The Advantages of Retail Arbitrage 178
Chapter 8 How to Pick the Right Products 184
Chapter 9 Find a supplier 197
Chapter 10 Contacting Suppliers 203
Chapter 11 All about Orders 205
Chapter 12 Affiliate Marketing 211
Chapter 13 Running Your Own Dropshipping Business 217
Chapter 14 Scaling Up Your FBA Business 224
Chapter 15 Avoiding Common Dropshipping Mistakes 231
Chapter 16 Tips for Succeeding with Your Online Business 234
Conclusion 241

DROPSHIPPING

DROP SHIPPING: A STEP-BY-STEP GUIDE FOR BEGINNERS TO BUILD A PASSIVE INCOME STREAM USING THE DROP SHIPPING BUSINESS MODEL FOCUSED ON E-COMMERCE MARKETING (SHOPIFY, AMAZON FBA, EBAY).

Description

Dropshipping has revolutionized the way we do business online. While it might sound intimidating to beginners, the fundamentals could not be simpler. The traditional methods of ecommerce are usually what we think of when selling items online. You advertise and market the item, buyers pay and leave their postal address, you package and send the item. While this might be great if you have all the time in the world to package and handle items, in today's fast paced world there has got to be an easier way.

This is where dropshipping takes the stage as the cornerstone of online business. The idea is simple yet unique. You advertise your item and buyers pay and leave their postal address, only this time instead of hassling with a warehouse of items to pack and send you simply leave the details of the items and the buyer's address with your designated drop shipper. The drop-shipper, from their much larger warehouse, then packs and sends the item on your behalf.

The beauty of this system is that you literally have the ability to make money without prior investment. Having no inventory to weigh you down is an immense benefit particularly in uncertain times since you will only ever pay for an item after a purchase has been made.

The entire business can be outsourced and automated after you get a hang of things. Customer service can be outsourced to several outsourcing companies or you could simply hire a virtual assistant or freelancer to do the job for you. A business manager can be hired from freelancing sites such as Fiverr or Upwork if you decide to completely automate the business and live off its passive income every month. But first let us go to the basics and fundamentals of the dropshipping business. Let us learn how to walk before we attempt to fly.

This guide will focus on the following:

- The advantages of working in dropshipping
- Getting ideas on what products to choose
- Finding the right niche
- Find and work with the right suppliers
- Building the website
- How to run your dropshipping company
- The dropshipping model of business
- Shopify dropshipping
- How to dropship on amazon and eBay
- Taking a look at current trends
- Social media approach in dropshipping... AND MORE!!!

Introduction

Have you ever stopped to consider just how online shopping works? It may seem obvious to you, but when you buy a product online, there are generally four ways in which a seller can deliver this product to your doorstep.

They ship the product to you themselves. In this instance, the seller has the product on hand, packages it themselves, and ships it to your address. This is probably the most obvious method for sellers to utilize, but it necessarily the best for all entrepreneurs.

It is a digital product, and there's no shipping required. This is a wonderful situation for an entrepreneur attempting to make sales online, but unless you're in the digital publishing or software business, there's a good chance this won't apply to you.

The seller originally purchased the product, but has a third-party fulfillment service that ships their goods. This is a growing trend. As space limitations and time limitations make it difficult for small teams (or even sole proprietors) to handle a large amount of shipping and handling on top of their other business requirements, services like Fulfillment by Amazon handle the process of shipping goods as they are sold. The seller still buys the product, so the investment in terms of cost is actually higher than shipping on your own, but often the time freed allows for scaling the business and working on finding new products and working on marketing rather than the labor of getting a package to a customer.

The seller lists a product they have not bought, and a supplier ships the product to the consumer when a sale is made. This is known as drop-shipping, and the initial investment on the part of the seller is much less than traditional sales. However, with drop shipping comes additional costs for products and often additional fees, meaning lower profit margins per sale. However, because initial investment is mostly time, this means that more risks can be taken on a large range of products, and scaling the business can begin almost immediately, rather than when funds allow for it. This makes drop shipping one of the premier methods for those getting started.

While drop shipping isn't by any means the only way to reach a six-figure ecommerce goal, it is perhaps the least stressful and the most open ended. For this reason, many of us in the ecommerce field begin here even if we eventually branch out into other forms of sales as well. For those of us that prefer to put in the time rather than the cost, such as having a limited budget to start with, it is perhaps the best possible method of becoming a success ecommerce entrepreneur.

Dropshipping is becoming an increasingly common way to do business online, taking the fundamentals of ecommerce but simply adding a middleman to take care of the shipping and supply. There is huge potential to make an impressive income if you remain focused and determined while keeping on top of managing your business. While you may not be spending time packing and sending orders, there is still plenty of work to do, though you will be mainly focused with sales and marketing to grow and expand your operations.

Your customer does not see you. You are a ghost in the entire operation. Every step of this drop shipping process can be done with just a laptop and a Wifi connection. There is huge potential when it comes to this lucrative business model. Firstly, you do not have to stock any products nor pay for product storage. Secondly, you will only pay for the product after your customer has paid for it. You are using part of your customer's money to pay for the product. The remaining amount will be your profit of course. Hence there is zero capital risk involved in the entire operation. Talk about a risk free investment. However, like all businesses, your time and effort is required to make this a success.

The Entrepreneur Frame of Mind

The entrepreneur frame of mind is an important aspect of any business, and while drop shipping doesn't require the type of investments that many other business models would require, having the frame of mind of a risk-taking entrepreneur is still an important facet of being successful.

We may not display all of these traits, but a balanced entrepreneur does possess at least some of the following traits:

Willing to take risks. For us, this means a lot of time. We are able to avoid some of the financial risk, but any time spent trying to earn money is time spent not earning money from a more traditional route.

Smart about their risk taking. While the risk may be there, that doesn't mean we just jump into any risky opportunity. Running a successful ecommerce business isn't simply about throwing a fistful of darts and hoping one hits the bullseye. Sure, that's an apt analogy for the general process, but we are throwing these darts with an attempt at precision rather than throwing them haphazardly.

Looks for opportunities constantly. This is what truly sets apart an entrepreneur from simply being a small business owner. A small business owner can open a business because the subject matter is one of the things they love in life. An entrepreneur may be so lucky, but they are also going to be constantly looking for a new opportunity, a way to get ahead of the game, and a way to improve upon what is already available on the market. While we won't always be creating our own products, we still have to take the time to SELL these products. Being innovative in our approach is key to growing our business to earn us a six-figure income.

Isn't afraid of a changing market... which is great, because all markets are constantly changing in the world of ecommerce. There are always going to be new players, and the big players are going to be trying to keep abreast of things BEFORE and WHILE they are trending.

Motivated! This is perhaps one of the hardest things to accomplish as an aspiring entrepreneur. You need a REASON to want to become financially independent. For some, simply being rich is enough, but for many, we need to take the time to create a goal that goes with that fortune. Why do you want a lot of money? Why are you willing to work your butt off for it? If you don't have anything to work hard for, then why even bother?

Sees past the money. This may sound crazy, but the approach shouldn't ONLY be "what makes money?" What makes money today may not make money tomorrow, so if you operate solely on what is worth money, you can very often miss the bigger picture about why consumers spend the way they do. What does the consumer care about? How do we fit into their needs? And only then, how does that translate to earnings?

At the end of the day, the main thing about having the entrepreneur state of mind is truly the dedication to invest your time and energy. If you are prone to false starts, then it is important to realize that no great idea is going to take off until you change how you operate. For some, we only succeed in the "make or break" moments of our lives, but for your sake, I urge you to realize that working a steady job and getting paid a mediocre wage SHOULD be enough to realize that you're already in the "make or break" stage, even if you're not about to bottom out anytime soon so long as you stay employed.

Do you really want to continue making a mediocre wage and giving 5 out of 7 days of your life to someone else's riches? It may be easier to auto-pilot through a job you don't like, but I can almost guarantee you will be happier if you work harder and pave your own path. I'll end my rant here!

How Exactly Does Dropshipping Work?

Going back to the topic at hand, drop shipping is a fairly simple concept, and while the process may vary slightly depending on sales channels and the suppliers you are working with, the general steps are always the say:

A manufacturer makes the product.

A supplier (sometimes the manufacturer) offers the product for wholesale prices.

A business owner (or sole proprietor) lists these products for sale on their website or through a third-part marketplace like Amazon or eBay. They do not buy the product themselves for the intention of shipping it to the consumer.

A consumer purchases the product from the seller.

The seller (or a piece of software) informs the supplier that a product has been sold and either pays for the product immediately or pays for all sold products at the end of the month.

The supplier ships this product to the consumer on the seller's behalf.

The seller keeps the profit after the cost of the product, shipping, and any relevant fees.

The consumer receives their item, usually none the wiser that the seller never actually touched it themselves.

This is the simple explanation of how drop shipping works. Of course, there are many facets to each step along the way. For our purposes, we'll focus on working on listing products and working with suppliers. That may seem like two simple things, but the considerations are vast.

Is It Really Profitable?

The short answer is, "Definitely." The long answer is that like any risk, profit will vary depending on how well execution is handled, consumer response, and of course, the initial cost of products and any service fees from the supplier or third-party marketplaces.

It is important to note that while drop shipping isn't as profitable on per-unit sales as other methods, the sheer ability to list as many products as you want without upfront costs means that it can be scaled to tremendous size even as a one-man team. Have a few people working together, and the possibilities are pretty much endless.

Where Do I Start?

The best place to start is with some bits of knowledge concerning the investment that is involved in working on a drop shipping business. While the investment in terms of capital isn't necessarily high, there are still other forms of investment required from an aspiring entrepreneur.

Chapter 1 The Advantages of Working in Drop shipping

Limited Investments to Start

One of the best qualities of beginning an online store presence with Drop shipping capabilities is that there doesn't need to be a huge investment to begin. As long as the fees and enrollments are tended to the whole system can be a rather low budget costing. One must create a simple budget that is feasible in their situation and become more aware of the earning potential. The truth is that the less investment you put in at the beginning the less profit that you will get back in the long run or over time. This is not always the case if you can play good in the game of e-commerce. When the business first makes their step into e-commerce they also need to know their limits of investments.

It's important to get the basic steps in first before you jump all in with all of your money on one product shipment or filling the inventory to have every piece because we have to remember that the buyers are going to be an important part as well.

Remember that there is competition around every corner so consider the fact that there are other businesses like yours that may be in the same profit regime. We do not want to set the limits too low that they will not sustain the business model or standards set out. Just because there can be a lost cost of entry the truth is that you may need to invest more than the bare minimum to begin making the profit e-commerce will bring. Do not be intimidated by the competition that will be alongside your product line because there is room for everyone in this e-commerce world.

Easy to Get Started

This is going to be a small financial risk that you have to take and have to gear up for which moves we are going to make to see revenue come to our business. There have to be urgent actions done for the great experience of the customers. Information and product descriptions are going to be the next second habit that you develop so that you can also ensure that you are a master of your craft. If you don't know everything about the product line that's okay, but we recommend that you have some extended background knowledge about the products in your inventory just in case you run into a problem with a customer that needs extended information on the product that you sold and shipped them.

Lots of Products to Choose From

You may be considering the products plentiful to you and maybe adding more and more to your inventory as we speak. Do not stack this tower too high or things will topple and your inventory can come crashing down. Don't be caught off guard with too much to hold and a crashing halt. When the company adds too much inventory to their business catalog, there can be a difficult time moving inventory out of the warehouse and this can become problematic.

Some inventory may not be selling at all, and there may be other problems with popularity or bad review of products you have in your inventory. There can be inventory that you have that individuals have purchased and left bad reviews about on other e-commerce websites. This is a business that you can do in a global market and that means that you are going to expand your market through countries and cities everywhere. Do not judge any avenue that you try to market towards and reach out to every potential prospect that you possibly can find and define a better demographic of buyers.

You are going to find customers that are looking for a steady supply of the product line you have and there are going to be one–time buyers that will help your profit. Every customer must be treated the same with importance and respect to ensure that everyone knows that you are a reputable establishment. One of the basic things you are going to need at all times is WiFi and you will be able to track your online business anywhere you are at using a self-made calendar and an optimized application made for your money services. This will create an urgent mindset for the business because some order will come in and they will need to be handled with some time sensitivity.

Be aware that you will be supplying customers with products that they may rely on for their business. This is why it is important to follow these simple steps to create a useful presence on the internet. The business has to be profitable in every way for there to be an enjoyable workflow. Follow your instincts with product choice and get ready to begin. You are just going to get geared up for a few extra steps you must take you may not have heard of before. This is where we are going to be thankful we don't own a whole warehouse we have to both staff and management. We are skipping the middleman and we are going to become the go-to for our shop's great experience.

It's a Business That You Can Do in a Global Market

Global e-commerce is going to be a new world and you are going to find that you are not alone here. There are going to be striving companies just like yours that need the same amount of attention and passion to achieve the success it entails. Just because there are other drop-shippers out there with you on the web that doesn't mean there needs to be competition between two corporations. No business should ever have to compete with a business like Amazon because there is room for everyone and there is the same general focus shared.

Since it is a global market you are going to be taking orders and making shipments at different times and different places. You can practically make sales overnight and have your product in full rotation by the time you wake up to have coffee the next morning. There aren't going to be an open and closing signs for your shop because it's going to have a 24/7 presence online and this is going to maximize all opportunities for profit. Recognize that you may need to even do some interpreting because customers will come from every walk of life to just have one of the products on your line today.

We just need to figure out the best way we are going to market to our global crowd and how we are going to create a likable and shareable space for everyone coming to visit. Use simplicity when choosing your marketing points for your new global crowd. Our buyers must share the same interests and find the same importance in the business that is online. There must be deep connections and feelings attached to the store, and this is going to increase reputation value in more than just the community downtown. It is important to reach out to the customers that will build our foundation because they will spread our name to their close ones and corporations.

When we can establish a connecting and trustworthy space for your customers it's going to bring their close ones as well to the sites you set and this will create a greater fan base for your products. Once there is a strong structure of customer traffic you will begin to receive reviews to your store and the products inside and this is going to connect even more customers in the world. Others will be able to see new reviews that your faithful customers are kindly leaving and this is going to attract new crowds to purchase the other inventory they are unaware of.

This is going to be a new load of work since you are marketing everywhere around the world, but you are going to see a return come to your business because this isn't going to be a normal community reach. The global market you create may solve problems that customers have had for years as long as you can be a trustworthy source of supply and you will be the only shop that they choose to go to.

Easy to Scale Up

You may not be able to afford everything that you are going to learn about if you are starting with a low budget. But this is why we are going to ramp up production simply by just beginning. You will find more and more forward motivation with the decision you decide to make and that includes every shipment. Once you are making consistent sales every week and you notice that orders are coming in annually you may want to consider scaling up your productions. Truth is that you most likely are not going to see sales immediately come in the first day and especially if you have done no extra marketing for your site.

Give it some time and you are going to see a great return. If you have a high end and popular item in your e-commerce inventory, then we can consider the fact that you may need to get ready for the number of customers you are going to have right from the start to your site. Do not be afraid to use all means of advertising which can include user applications and social media to your advantage. Remember that you are going to scale up your store's traffic and that is going to mean finding a specific buyer crowd that has targeted interests. Look into blogs and forums that have other individuals asking frequent questions and give them helpful links to your store and see where it will get the business.

You are going to be an e-commerce shop that supplies the everyday individual and they couldn't need just a few units, but maybe a hundred units from your store. We are going to need to ramp up inventory capacity and find new ways to keep up with the demand of the customers that trust the businesses services. You may be selling a hundred or two hundred units a day and this will be because they are not high value enough to see a high return on. This will make your profits come in slower, but you will still profit nonetheless and we have to remember how much work this would be for one person every day if there were no warehouse with employees to make magic happen. Moving hundreds of units every day is going to take work and we have to be honest about this.

Easy to Automate

There are customers in other cities that will need your products on time advanced schedules and you can automate recurring shipments and this can give you so much time to do your other Drop shipping duties. Remember that there are tools that can do exactly what you have been asking for. We have to consider all of the ways that automating your services with other services is going to create a stable structure for learning about perfecting this craft.

Create templates that export sales orders using drop shipping systems. The inserted templates will then auto-populate when an order is received on whatever marketplaces or shop checkouts that the business deal with. It'll then be forwarded to your supplier as an email with a CSV attachment and this is going to act as an internal invoice. There will be agreements and surely; even a negotiated contractual agreements that assure the services provided will be fulfilled as well. Shortly after the order will be fulfilled, and all information that is about the product and package will be sent to the buyer for confirmation. This process can be done while the business owner is tending to other tasks unrelated without even having to opening an app or check in and out of tedious tasks.

VA's are a good way to go for a good way to manage your order fulfillment, and all you have to do is be one or you can hire one. Marketing agencies can handle your advertising presence online or in person, and there can even be a possible web developer hired and as well some electronic customer support system that you know the customers will be happy with in case running into any problem. Remember that you are going to be handling a lot in the beginning phases of the e-commerce shop so it may not be the easiest thing to dive completely into automated Dropshipping.

It is recommended that the business owner can get used to handling and shipping the products using every trial and error so that the process is all acquainted. We need to also understand that it's not necessary to automate your drop shipping system early so that you are trying to move out the entire inventory you have out the door in complete stress. The most cost efficient tactic the business can take for their online automation is critical, but we must make sure are all aware of the exact duties we must fulfill to run a successful online shop.

It is best to do the most you can with your e-commerce business on your own. You are going to learn a lot of dos and don'ts of your business and have full control of your business. There must be full control of the business so that you are not on the sidelines and unaware of any random occurrences. A dedicated owner is going to be at the front lines of their business and the customers are going to see it with trust. Your profit will be higher with a promise to expand even further with your global presence. Of course, this all only applies if you are in a growth/startup phase and you are at least somewhat able to do these tasks on your own.

Remember that you are going to be spending money on these services to automate the drop shipping done for your e-commerce store. Nothing is free, but there are some pretty decent rates as long as you find all of your options online before you make that choice with your trusted company. You are going to be spending money to do your business and it may seem like money is coming and in without balance, but it's your job to truly make sure that you are receiving pure profit if not breaking even to meet your monthly income plan.

Chapter 2 Getting Ideas on What Products to Choose

By now you should have a list of products that you would like to sell. If you haven't found a separate list of items that are trending, go through social media to find what people are talking about. You can also do a search online of the Top 10 Drop shipping Websites and check them out to see what they are featuring. You should always know what your competitors are doing anyway, from what they are selling, to what they are charging, and what they are not selling.

Check out social shopping sites, like Etsy and Pinterest, to see what is trending. You will quickly be able to see which products are getting the most attention. You will also be able to see what items are being shared and recommended.

Whenever you are checking out any products, some of the most invaluable information you can get is through the testimonials from those who have already paid and purchased these products. They can give you the pros and cons as well as alert you to potential shipping and customer service issues they experienced.

Wanelo.com is another excellent source of information. You can browse through a vast array of some of the best online stores from this single site. There are a number of different ecommerce businesses that are carrying a wide variety of products.

If you are a part of any specific groups, clubs, or support blogs online, check out to see what people are talking about. This, along with reviews and testimonials, will give you some of the most honest feedback on what people are loving and items that didn't live up to the hype.

Lastly, when in doubt, search it out. Enter a search for Top Dropshipping Products for 2019 and see what pops up on the list. You can do this for any specific products, for example, you can find out how successful skincare products would be in your Drop shipping business. After entering this search it showed that this category turned out to be one of the most profitable niches on ecommerce in 2018. Take advantage of all of the information you have at your fingertips through the Internet. All you have to do is enter a question you want to be answered and phrase it exactly as if you were asking a friend. You will be surprised to have the answer to your question returned to you in a matter of minutes.

Establishing Your Criteria for Product Selection

As you get closer to finding products you would like to sell, you should begin to set up the criteria that each product must adhere to in order to be selected.

1. Popularity. You should completely research a product to see if it is trending, and if it is, is it at the beginning or end of its run. Even if it is trending, it may not be worth it by the time you add it to your product line.
2. Price. What is the retail price for this item? Is it available as a wholesale item? What are my competitors selling the same item for? You may want to set up a section for low-priced items and higher priced products. Each group will attract a different clientele but it may let you know that it

is easier to deal with higher-priced items than go for low-costing products.
3. Profit margin. Once you find a price for each product that you are comfortable with, you will have to adjust each one so that you can reach the amount you need to make the profit you set up for your business.
4. Repeat business. Is this a product that will automatically require repeat business? This could affect the price as it might make up for percentages if it made it up in ongoing volume. This could give you a small but regular income.
5. Target market. You must identify the type of people who will not only be interested in each product, but who will be willing to enter their credit card info so they can make a definite purchase. You wouldn't expect people who have a family that consists of small children to be interested in the same things as single millennials. Knowing your audience will definitely help you make more sales.

What are Restricted Brands?

When you are working through Amazon, they have a list of restricted brands that you are not allowed to sell on their site. Amazon restricts certain brands for several different reasons.

1. They are trying to keep counterfeit items from being sold on their site.
2. The company that has the products may already have exclusivity with Amazon.

3. The company may have exclusivity with an Amazon seller or sellers already

You will need approval to sell a restricted brand on Amazon. If you do get approval, it does not automatically mean you can sell all the items in a particular category. Counterfeit products are a very serious and expansive issue with Amazon. Instead of giving approval on certain restricted brands they make the sellers by these products directly from the manufacturer. You would have to be listed as a reseller who is authorized to do so. You wouldn't even be able to show or list these items on Amazon without prior approval. Some items may be okay to sell but only if they are in the used category. There are ways that you can deal with this situation more easily. It includes Retail Arbitrage.

What is Retail Arbitrage?

While the name sounds complicated, the process is very simple. Retail arbitrage is a process where a store, usually one that sells items at discounted prices, has items either in their store or on their website that you are able to buy at a very low price. You purchase the items at this deeply discounted price and resell it at a higher price and you will probably made a very good profit on the deal.

You may have read about a sharp businessman or two who got into the practice of physically going to stores like Walmart or Target and bought up as many sale or clearance items as they could and then resold the items online making enough of a profit that they were able to quit their regular full-time jobs.

Many times people wonder if the deal is so great, why don't the stores just sell the items themselves and make their own money back? The reason is these stores are so big with lots of inventory they often need the room and it is easier for them to just get the products out the door so they can bring in higher-priced items.

Retail arbitrage is allowed on Amazon but there are steps that must be in place. You probably wonder why potential customers don't just go into the stores themselves and buy the products as cheaply as you are. One of the reasons is that prices are not always the same at every major store across the country. A Walmart in Florida may not have those discounted items in one of their stores in Tennessee.

With the convenience of Amazon Prime offering 2-day, next day, and even same-day delivery, more people every day are shopping from the comfort of their homes.

If you are going forward with retail arbitrage it is recommended that you make sure you have the app for Amazon Seller on your phone or laptop. This will allow you to check to see if a product you are interested in selling is on the restricted list. Once you enter the name of the product you will be able to see if you can sell the item as well as what condition it has to be in for you to sell it – new or used.

There is an extension you have to have on your computer if you are looking for Items to resell online. When you open the AZIsight Chrome browser on your computer and you get to the product page on Amazon, you will be able to see right away if the item is restricted or not. This app is very comprehensive and will not only show you if the item is restricted, it will direct you right to a page where you can ask for permission to sell the item without even leaving the site.

Selling on Amazon will be a much smoother process if you go to the Seller Central screen and sign on to get the approval process started. You have to meet the requirements that

Amazon has in place and be approved so you are able to sell products in specific categories.

Is Retail Arbitrage for You?

Retail Arbitrage is another way to make a decent amount of money through ecommerce. Instead of sourcing specific products, you are buying items that are deeply discounted as they appear in certain stores or online. You may have to physically go to the store that has the items so you can feature them on your site.

Amazon has been cited as being one of the best places to conduct retail arbitrage. The first thing you will have to do is sign up for a seller account on Amazon. You can sign up for an individual but may want to convert to an individual seller account. It will only take a few minutes to get signed up and once you do you will be able to utilize the free app that is available and will help you source your products.

The only app you need to start your retail arbitrage business is the Amazon Seller App. There is no charge for this app but it will give you valuable information. Once you are signed up you can scan barcodes with the camera you have on your cell phone. Once you do this you will be able to find out how much the item is selling for on Amazon and what the fees and costs are for each item you scan. This app will provide you will all the information you need to determine whether putting a specific item for sale will be worth it.

What you will need to know before you conduct the search is what the minimum amount is that you need to make on each item in order to make a profit. If the amount shown on the site is less than that amount you shouldn't even waste your time listing it. It is suggested that you aim for a return on investment (ROI) of more than 50 percent in order to become profitable.

When deciding on buying items for retail arbitrage, too much of a good thing isn't always a good thing. Keep your purchases of really good deals on the lower side. Depending on the item, things can change quickly online and you might make out okay on the first few sales but if prices drop unexpectedly you might lose money instead of make money.

Once you have your products purchased and ready to sell on Amazon you will want to enlist the Fulfillment by Amazon program. Once you send your products in bulk to them, they will, in turn, take care of sending all of the sold items to the corresponding customers. Fulfillment by Amazon has locations where they will store the items and ship them out to your customers as they are purchased. At the end of this book, you will find a list of the top stores to use for retail arbitrage using Amazon FBA.

Choosing Your Niche Category and Market

A common phrase that was used when choosing to embark on a career was to find your niche. In this case, it means a specific area that you feel comfortable in, have a passion for and are ready to make this area define you. If you love to cook, that is a broad category but if you love to cook Italian food, this would be your niche.

In the world of ecommerce, finding your niche category does have something to do with finding an area you are passionate about. When you are passionate about a subject you will naturally become knowledgeable in it and become something of an expert.

Finding your niche market is where you find a specific segment of a market, there is a problem that needs to be solved, and there is a large demand for the product but a slim supply. When you find something that fits these criteria, you will usually have an ecommerce item that could be a profitable item for your product line.

If you are serious about your Drop shipping business you have to put the time in to determine what your niche category is. This step will help to solidify your chances of success as you begin to sell items online.

So, how do you go about finding and defining your niche? There are several steps you can take to get a handle on your niche category so you can develop and expand your niche market.

10 Steps You Can Take to Choose Your Niche Category

- Make a list of all the things that you are most interested in.

The list could also contain any areas that you are most knowledgeable in. When you are interested in things and passionate about them your enthusiasm will be contagious and will draw customers to you who enjoy the same things. This would bring a receptive audience right to your site who would be primed and ready to buy the products you are excited about and are sharing with them.

This could start off as simply as how much you love your dog. If your dog is a specific breed he may have special needs or need or enjoy certain types of products that you could offer on your site. You may become recognized for being an authority on this type of dog and word of mouth, the best type of advertising, will bring you many new customers.

- Check out Amazon to see what the top-selling items are.

Keep an eye on Amazon because their information is updated every hour. If you pay attention and put the time in you just might be lucky enough to be in the right place at the right time,

- Open your eyes and your mind to everything you see.

Pay attention to what you see on television, what your friends are talking about, what the most popular items people seem to be buying, and what is trending on social media.

- Think of any problems that you think could be solved.

So many great ideas show up on shows like The Shark Tank. When we watch the people who appear on that show with a novel idea, we all wonder the same thing: "Why didn't I think of that?" Many of the ideas that do get the sharks to invest go on sale to the public a short time later.

- Don't overlook niche areas that will always be relevant.

When you are looking for just the right niche category for your niche market, there are a host of areas that will never go out of style that will always be able to provide you with products to source for your business.

These include:

- Weight loss items

Diet books – both old and new. There are many tried and true programs that are still relevant after years on the market.

- Exercise programs and equipment

These change regularly but things like yoga, walking, weight training, and running always have new information and most have the equipment required to get the best results.

- Cooking

This area has exploded and besides an entire network devoted to food, there are ethnic foods that never seem to lose their popularity as well as new trends that focus on getting dinner on the table in 15 minutes or less. Besides cookbooks, there are unlimited kitchen gadgets that pop up and people can't get enough of - a zoodler? A good set of pots and pans never goes out of style but there is always the gadget of the moment, such as The Instant Pot.

- Appearance and Personal Grooming

In 2018, cosmetics and skincare were some of the top sourced products on the ecommerce scene. Everyone always wants to look their best as well as stay looking as young as they can for as long as they can. Having beautiful hair, the whitest teeth, and the smoothest skin are always a priority for most people and there is never a lack of attention in this category.

- The Animal Kingdom

We love our pets. There is even an ad for a certain pet food whose motto is "Love them like family. Feed them like family." With that in mind, there is an abundance of products people will spend money on because they love their pets so much. They will plunk down their hard-earned money on everything from squeak toys to sweaters for their dogs to wear in the winter. And don't forget boots so their feet don't get cold.

- Family Life

Whether your child is 15 minutes old or 15 years old, there is no end to the things they need, want or just have to have. There are old standbys, like Legos and coloring books, and then there are new items, such as slime, the ever-popular video games, and of course, phones for the entire family always have to be up-to-date.

- Home is where the heart is.

Along with the ever-trending food shows, do-it-yourself projects and homes you buy so you can fix them up and sell them at a profit are the next best thing. There are Youtube videos for everything so it follows that after viewing a DIY project you will need the tools and items to bring that project to fruition.

- Look for items that have a price tag that is on the higher end.

If you take finding your niche market seriously and put the time in you will end up working smart instead of hard. Don't be afraid to go after items that are more expensive. You have a chance of making a higher profit margin with high-end products.

- **Clothing and Accessories**

Fashions may change every season but you don't have to go to Fashion Week to know what's in style. Check out as many clothing websites as you can, browse through fashion magazines, and just look around to see what people are wearing because that is what they are buying. Pay attention and make sure to jump on the latest trend as soon as you can because it could be over before you know it. Who would have thought that jeans that are torn up all over would be a fashion statement? Just make sure you don't act on anything that appears because you think you are going to make a fortune on it. Onesies and dresses for men have never taken off in the real world even though they keep trying.

Chapter 3 Finding the right niche

Niche research and product selection are among the most important steps in building a successful drop shipping business. There are no other ways around them. You have to do them if you want to increase your chances for achieving sustained profitability. I'm telling you right now that niche research takes time and effort. It can take you days or even weeks to zero in on products that you think will be embraced by customers. Niche research is about gathering data and gauging demand for your product ideas. In other words, it's a strategy for determining if it's worth it to pursue a product or not.

What is a Niche?

In the simplest of terms, a niche is a specific category or field in an industry. This is in business and marketing terms. For example, let's talk about the broad outdoor equipment industry. Under this industry are dozens of niches. The trail running community is a niche. The mountain climbing community is a niche. The cliff jumping community is a niche. The mountain biking community is yet another niche. And so on and so forth. Even these niches can be further broken down into even smaller niches. For example, the trail running community niche can be broken down into the marathoner's niche and the ultra-marathoner's niche.

Breaking down an industry into niches makes it a lot easier for aspiring entrepreneurs to find potential markets they can tap into. It allows you to look for niches that have less competition but have considerable demand. These are the two factors that you must always consider during niche research. One, the competition within the niche shouldn't be too tough in the sense that you can enter it and carve your own business in it. And two, there should be considerable demand for the products you want to offer in that niche. These two factors come hand in hand. Because what's the point of entering an uncompetitive niche if there's minimal demand for products. And what's the point of trying to fulfill a demand that's already being fulfilled by thousands of established entrepreneurs – profit margins will erode due to too much competition.

How to do Niche Research

Always remember that you have two main goals when performing niche research. One, you want to gauge demand for your product ideas. And two, you want to know the level of competition for those product ideas. You will be performing most of your research using various tools like keyword research tools and search volume trackers. Don't worry because most of these tools and resources are readily available and you can use most of them for free. Before you begin with your research, it's important that you already have an industry that you want to target. For example, you want to target the sports gear industry or the weight loss industry. I hope that you are getting my point here. The general industry serves as your starting point.

Create a Quick List of Your Product Ideas
The first thing you must do is write down a quick list of the products that you have in mind. Get a piece of paper and quickly jot down the ideas. This list will be your reference point when you start doing your research. Write down the words, phrases, and terms that come to your mind when you think about your potential products. Allow me to briefly illustrate what this list should look like. Let's say that you want to build a drop shipping business around the hiking

niche. Furthermore, let's say that you want to sell hiking footwear on your drop shipping website. Brainstorming for product ideas, your initial list should look very similar to the following list:

- Hiking shoes
- Hiking sandals
- Mountain climbing shoes
- Hiking footwear
- Climbing sandals
- Durable climbing shoes
- Hiking slippers
- Tough hiking shoes
- Mountaineering shoes
- Mountaineering footwear
- Mountaineering sandals

This is just for illustration purposes. Your list can either be shorter or longer than the one above. It all depends on the products you have in mind and the niche that you want to target. My main point here is that you need to create a list of all your potential products. These should be the types of products that you plan on selling through your drop shipping website. Creating this list should take just a few minutes of your time. Some drop-shippers would even divide their lists into product categories and create lists within a list. Keep a copy of this list with you as you start with your niche research.

Google Is Your Best Friend

Google controls at least 60% of all online searches so it makes sense that the search giant has the most accurate search data and statistics. Needless to say, if you want to learn about a product's popularity online, Google is where you should go for information. Google has tools that you can use for your research. The two most important ones are *Google Trends* and the *Google Keyword Tool*. Don't worry, both of these tools are free to use. You don't have to pay a dime to gain access to their features and functions. For the Keyword Tool, all you need is a Google account. If you already have a Gmail account, you can start using the Keyword Tool by simply logging into your account.

For the Google Trends tool, you don't even need a Google account to access and use it. For best results, I suggest that you use the Chrome browser when you do your research on Google Trends. Certain features of the tool tend to not work properly when you use other browsers like Mozilla Firefox. Google Trends is a very powerful research tool in the sense that you can determine search volume over time, top and rising search terms, seasonality of search terms, and even the geographical concentrations of searches. You can identify which countries are searching the most for particular products. In the following sections, I'm going to show you how to use the two tools.

How to Use Google Trends for Niche Research

Here's a quick definition of Google Trends from Wikipedia: "It is a public web facility of Google based on Google Search that shows how often a particular search term is entered relative to the total search volume across different regions in the world, and in various languages." It's basically an analytics database of all searches on Google from 2004 to the present. Needless to say, Google Trends is a goldmine for data about ecommerce niches. It contains an immense amount of search data that you can collect and analyses to determine if there's interest or demand for the products that you have in mind.

Let's take a look at the tool's specific features:

☐ *Interest and Search Volume over Time* – This graphs searches based on the queries they received over time. You can quickly customize a time frame ranging from years to minutes. The graph will show you if the search volume for a particular search query is increasing or decreasing over time. It provides you with an idea if the trends will be in your favor or not. Let's say that you are planning to dropship trail running shoes. Google Trends will provide you with data if searches for the phrase "trail running shoes" is increasing or decreasing over time. If the trend shows that the number of people interested in trail running shoes is growing, then it's probably a good niche and that it's worth looking into. You can compare search data based on time periods. For example, you can compare search data this year to last year's search data. Or you can compare search data this month to last month's search data.

☐ *Interest by Region* – This feature enables you to pinpoint the geographical regions wherein your search term is most popular. It compares the origins of the searches. The interest data also reflects the popularity of the term in a certain region and on a certain time period. For example, you want to know more about the interest for "trail running shoes" during the first quarter of 2018. That's for the months of January, February, and March. What you do is customize the parameters in Google Trends so that it will reflect interest about "trail running shoes" during these months.

The data will then show you the regions where queries for "trail running shoes" are most popular.

However, you should take note that the geographic regions are organized based on search proportions. Needless to say, some smaller countries might score much higher compared to larger countries. Interest for searches is scored by Google Trends from 0 to 100. You can determine search interest not just by country. You can further break down the interest data by states or provinces. For example, if you are doing research in the United States, you can access interest data by state.

☐   *Related Topics* – What this feature does is providing a quick list of other topics that the user also searched. Users searching for your term are also searching for these terms and topics. In our example, if you input "trail running shoes" into Google Trends, the related topics that you receive include the following topics: vapor, venture 6, sports shoes, tights, cross training, track spikes, back country running, vibram, under armor. This means that whoever is searching about trail running shoes are also interested in these general topics. How does this benefit you in your research for a niche? Well, it provides you with a ton of ideas about other products that your target market might be interested in. From our example, we can see that people searching for trail running shoes are also interested in running shorts and running spikes. These are products that you might also want to feature in your drop shipping store.

☐   *Related Queries* – A lot of people often confuse this with the Related Topics feature. The two are very different from each other. In Related Topics, you get a list of topics that the user also searched for. This means that these are general topics. In Related Queries, you are presented with a list of terms that the user also searched for. This means that people searching for your main term are also searching for these queries. In other words, these are specific queries. In our example on trial running shoes, the user also searched for the following queries: best trail running shoes 2018, black and yellow running shoes, file trail running shoes, brooks Cascadia, zero drop running shoes, best waterproof trail running shoes, Salomon speed cross 4, best trail running shoes women, and trail running shoes for hiking. These are very specific queries that the user is also searching for. Again, how will this information help you with your niche research? My answer is the same. The information helps you with more ideas about which products to promote and sell. It also provides you with ideas about other niches that you might want to further explore.

☐ *Top vs. Rising Queries* – When you look at the list of queries and topics under the Related Topics and Related Queries features, you can toggle the terms between Top and Rising. In Related Topics, the Top designation refers to the most popular topics. The Rising designation refers to topics with the largest increase in search frequency since the previous time period. In Related Queries, the Top designation refers to the most popular search queries. The Rising designation refers to search queries with the largest increase in search frequency since the previous time period. The data you gather from these features paint a picture of what's currently popular and what topics and terms have the potential to become popular.

☐ *Breakout Search Queries* – This is a feature which identifies whether a topic or a query is receiving a breakout number of searches. A topic or query is tagged as a "breakout" if there is a tremendous increase in interest and search volume for it. For example, if the search volume for "zero drop running shoes" last week was in the mere hundreds but during the current week the search volume ballooned to searches in the thousands. It will most likely be tagged as a "breakout" topic or query. However, you should be careful about breakout topics and queries because these are usually seasonal in nature. This is especially true for products that are seasonal. For example, Christmas sweaters are often tagged as breakout topics and queries weeks before Christmas day. For sure, it would be a good idea to start drop shipping Christmas sweaters but the interest will quickly die out within a month or so. If you want to build a sustainable drop shipping business that is profitable all year round, you should target products that are not seasonal in nature.

How to Download the Graphs and Data from Google Trends

On the top portion of each feature are buttons signifying actions you can take. Find the one that looks like an arrow pointing downwards. This is the universal symbol for "download". If you hover over it, it says "CSV". Just click on the button to commence downloading. Downloading will take just a few seconds. To open the file, just go to your desktop's "Downloads" folder. You can also embed the graphs from Google Trends. Just click on the Embed button and you will be provided with HTML code which you can just copy and paste into any page that supports HTML.

In a nutshell, Google Trends has almost everything you need to look for a profitable niche for your drop shipping business idea. For most experienced drop-shippers, Google Trends is all they need to find the next product they are going to sell. But if you are just a beginner, the data and information you collected from Google Trends may not be enough. That brings us to the Google Keyword Tool. If you are a complete newbie, I suggest that you make use of both tools in researching for your niche products.

Things to Look Out for When Selecting Products

Now that you have a good list of keywords related to the niche you want to enter, the next step is to zero in on the products that you are going to sell on your drop shipping website. There are several factors that you must consider, the most important of which are as follows:

1. *Price* – When drop shipping products, your prices should be competitive. It shouldn't be too high or too low. If it's too high, people will say it's overpriced. If it's too low, people will assume that your product is of low quality thus the low price. Most of the time, your customers are people who are too lazy to go out and buy the product themselves from department stores or groceries. So it's okay to dropship products at a slightly higher price compared to department store prices. Most consumers will understand the difference in the price.

When you look at the price of a product, you have to consider the markup associated with the drop shipping model. For example, if a pair of shoes you are planning to sell costs $20 on a retailer's ecommerce store, you have to assume that if you are going to dropship the same product, it will have to cost a little bit more. The markup should not be too much in the sense that the gap between your price and the other retailer's price is too much for the customer to justify.

2. *Marketing potential* – The product should be an item that can be marketed online on most promotional platforms. You should be able to promote it via social media, blogs, forums, direct advertising, content marketing, advertising programs like AdSense, podcasts, etc. Your target customers are online and the only way to reach them is through online marketing

channels. For this to work, the product has to be marketable on such a platform.

3. *Lots of related accessories* – As a drop-shipper, you have the option of selling accessories that are related to your main product. Accessories are a great source of additional sales and income. In fact, some drop-shippers make more money from their accessories than from their main products. The term "accessory" is a rather broad term so allow me to explain it further in the context of the drop shipping business model. Let us go back to our example of drop shipping trail running shoes. Accessories that you can sell which are relevant to your main product may include the following:

- Trail running socks
- Shoe gaiters
- Shoe blinkers
- Shoe glue
- Anti-blister socks
- Five finger socks

Adding accessories to your ecommerce store is a great idea. They are usually a lot less expensive so they get bought much quicker. And not to mention the fact that they are easier to pack and ship. You can also try to sell accessories in bundles or packages. Use these packages to entice your target customers to purchase your main products.

4. *Low Return Rate* – It's far more strategic to deal with products that are simple in nature in order to minimize the chance of something going wrong e.g. one would expect to see a higher return rate when drop shipping a fragile ceramic plate which is more likely to break on transit, especially if it's

packaged properly. Furthermore, electronic appliances are likely to malfunction which might lead customers to return them. However, dealing with simple products like a shoe, T-shirt, tennis ball, phone leather/rubber case etc. isn't quite as risky. As a result, it's easier to meet customer expectations and you're less likely to get unsatisfied customers asking for a refund.

5. *Hard to find locally* – Look for products that are rarely sold in department stores and grocery stores in your area. This is a good strategy especially if you are planning to dropship products to a specific location. For example, if trail running shoes are difficult to find in your town or city, then it would be a good idea to set up a drop shipping business selling trail running shoes and targeting customers in your town or city.

A Quick Recap of Measuring Competition

As I have mentioned several times already, you need to gauge the competition for a product before you decide to add the item to your drop shipping business. The general consensus is that if the competition is very tough, you should abandon the idea and brainstorm for others. This is true in many levels but there is an exception. Don't abandon the idea entirely. The fact that the competition for the product is very tough means that there's a lot of money to be made with the product. What you should do is further break down the product idea into niches and finds the ones with less competition. This way, you are within a competitive niche but you are targeting a product with less competition niche-wise. Doing so basically allows you to take advantage of the demand while avoiding too much competition.

Another powerful way of gauging competition is by examining the number of organically listed sites on the first page of Google. Type in your main keyword and analyses the results. If several pages of the results contain the exact keyword, then it's a very competitive niche – these many people wouldn't be running ads if there weren't money to be made. Look at the top results and think if you can compete with them. Do you think you can optimize your drop shipping website and make it rank high in the results page? Or are the top results too established that it would be nearly impossible to reach or even topple them? You have to be realistic with your analysis especially if there are a lot of big brands in the top search results. For example, you are overconfident if you think that you can compete with the likes of Nike or Adidas when it comes to selling running shoes online. They have a lot of marketing power and a sizeable budget. You have to avoid competing against the big dogs by finding your own niche.

Find a Niche Where You Can Add Value to the Product

One way of getting ahead of the competition is to add value to the products you are dropshipping. This is especially true if you are selling a generic product (one that is also being sold by countless other drop-shippers). Differentiate your business by creating a unique value proposition. The next obvious question is how do you do this? One of the best ways to add value to a competitive product is to create a loyalty program for your customers. This is a great strategy if the product you are drop shipping has a high turnover rate. What you do is reward you're most loyal customers in the form of discounts and promos.

Another great way of adding value to a product is to offer discounts for bulk purchases. A good example of this is a buy one take one sales model. It provides customers with a nice incentive that is too hard to refuse. Your customers will be getting more of your products at fewer costs. For this sales model to work, you also need to negotiate with your supplier or manufacturer for lesser costs when it comes to bulk orders. You can also arrange to bundle complementary products your customers will like to buy together e.g. a tennis ball and a racket, shoe and socks of matching brands, phones and phone cases etc.

Another method of adding value to your product is to customize its design and packaging. Beautiful packaging creates additional perceived value in the eyes of your customers. When a customer looks at your product, the very first thing they see and feel is the quality of the packaging. Having a good product design could make the whole difference between a buyer and a non-buyer. Making the product packaging as attractive as possible helps in making the customer decide to purchase the item.

Chapter 4 Find and Work with the Right Suppliers

After you have chosen the products to sell you need to decide the source from where you can get them. You can make a list of the products and their sources using Air-Table or Google Sheets. This can serve as one database for future reference.

The supplier plays a vital role in the drop shipping model of business. He forms the crux of the entire enterprise. Therefore it is important to find a supplier who does his work properly and fulfills the orders in a punctual and efficient manner.

Choosing a supplier is the most critical step towards establishing a successful business. If a supplier messes up the orders you will be held responsible for it. Try to find a reliable vendor to supply your goods.

Criteria for Choosing a Supplier for Dropshipping

It is necessary to keep these points in mind while selecting a supplier:

Look for experienced drop ship suppliers who have cooperative sales representatives: Using the services of an experienced supplier is the best option because he will be familiar with the pitfalls and will be in a position to tackle them more efficiently. Along with this if he has obliging sales representatives who are willing to answer all the questions you will have an excellent team. This will have a positive impact on your enterprise.

Try to find a supplier who provides good quality products: If the quality of the products is good the customers will be more satisfied and less items will be returned. Your products will get good reviews and feedback from them. Testimonials will give a boost to your business. So it is imperative to supply products of high quality.

Request the suppliers to provide product samples so that you can test the quality before entering into a partnership with them. Ideally, the supplier must provide good quality images which you can put up in the listings of products.

Search for a supplier with technological abilities: While choosing a supplier ensure that he has the technological capacity to keep pace with the new changes. He should be able to grow along with the progress of your business. There should be no need to break a partnership with the supplier when you scale the enterprise.

Find a supplier who can do the shipping efficiently and punctually: If your supplier can ship the products within 24 to 48 hours you can ensure that your customers are happy. There is a lot of competition in the market. So if the shipping times are too long customers may not find your service very attractive.

It is a good idea to order some items from your prospective supplier and test how he fulfills the order so that you can take a well informed decision.

He should be able to communicate properly: Mostly the suppliers are in far off places or overseas. So communication is very important. The suppliers should comprehend the orders correctly and respond quickly. You must be absolutely sure about the capacity of a supplier to communicate properly before you choose one.

He should provide the facility to drop ship the items: All the suppliers of products do not offer the service of drop shipping the goods. Some of them are only manufacturers or wholesalers. So before contacting any of them, make sure that they do the work of dropshipping.

His fees should not be very high: Usually, the drop ship suppliers charge a minimum fee for this service. This is fair enough as they keep the stock for you and organize the packing and shipping part of the transaction. However, the fees should be around 2 or 5 dollars only. Do not select a supplier who charges more than this amount.

Offer fast shipping: Mostly the drop ship suppliers are stationed in China. It is not possible to expect instant shipping. But you can see to it that the goods are delivered as quickly as possible. See how much time they take to ship the goods to various countries. If it is between 1 to 2 weeks it is acceptable. In case, it is longer than this you may receive negative feedback from your customers.

Provide referrals: Good suppliers should be willing to allow you to connect to businesses to verify if their service is up to the mark or not. You should get a confirmation from other businessmen about their service.

How to Find Dropship Suppliers

You can use Google to search for suppliers. The search results show many e-commerce websites and startup incubators which contain complete directories and contact information of the suppliers. After you get the details of the suppliers who offer the products which you wish to sell, send short courteous emails to them asking some pertinent questions. This will help you to fathom how obliging their sales representatives are and know how swiftly they respond.

You may not know at the very outset whether a supplier is the right fit or not. But you can ask certain questions which will help you to make the screening procedure more efficient.

Screening Process

Here are a few questions that can be asked in the first email. Choose any 3 of them so that it is not very overwhelming for your prospective supplier.

- Are you ready to manufacture customized products if needed?
- Let me know your prices. Can they be negotiated?
- Do you charge anything extra other than direct costs? (Ensure that no hidden costs are there)
- Do you provide the facility to return goods? What is your return policy?
- Do you perform the functions of a retailer or direct seller as well?
- What is the profit margin that can be expected?
- Do the prices fluctuate at any time?
- Is there a guarantee or warranty offered for the products?
- Is there some dedicated representative at your end who will clear all my doubts?
- Do you possess and make use of one data feed?

These questions will show the supplier that you are going to take a well informed decision. So he will not try to cheat you or misuse the fact that you are a newbie. In drop shipping the relationship between a retailer and supplier exists for a long time so there is a need for some commitment.

Find Legitimate Suppliers

In order to avoid becoming a target of scams it is necessary to take these steps:

Make use of some online tools and check the domain's age: This will enable you to cross-check all the claims of the supplier with the facts. If the domain is very new it could be a scam. Besides this, if you check the age of the domain you will get to know the level of experience of the supplier online.

Check the reviews about that supplier online: In case, the supplier has cheated someone earlier the victim may have posted some warning message or a negative review about him. However, it is possible to manipulate the online reviews.

See if the supplier's business is registered or not: It is important to find out if the supplier's business is registered. You must confirm that the address given for his warehouse or office is listed as some commercial space or business place. If the search results show that it is a residential space it may not be a good indication.

Contact the particular manufacturer directly and cross-check the facts: You can contact the manufacturer if you are not 100% sure about him. But you should be careful because if the scam is a big one, the pseudo manufacturer may also be a part of it.

You can read various business blogs where the entrepreneurs discuss dropshipping. You can learn from their experience in this field.

Spot Fake Dropshipping Suppliers

There are a number of drop shipping scams which should be avoided. Watch out for the red flags and safeguard your enterprise from them. For example, if a supplier does not agree to take checks and accepts bank transfers only, it could be one warning sign.

A fraudulent supplier will not provide his address on the website or in his business correspondence. A legitimate supplier must display his address. Moreover, many scams involve a "membership fee." Though this practice might not be deceitful at all times, conducting a thorough research is highly recommended in such cases.

After you have asked the appropriate questions, taken due precautions and done the research you should be able to find the supplier who is the right fit for your business. With this you would have completed a major step in setting up your business. Next you can concentrate on establishing a system to run the daily operations smoothly.

Options for Paying the Dropship Suppliers

You can pay the supplier for the things ordered by the customer within 15 to 45 days. The products will be shipped immediately but you will pay for it later.

Otherwise you can chose the pre-pay option. That means you will pay the money soon after submitting the order.

Payment Methods
Credit card: This is the best way to pre-pay the money. The supplier deducts the amount from your card when the order is submitted.

Debit card: You can use one debit card to pre-pay the cost of the order. But there may be some suppliers who do not accept this method.

Dwolla: If a supplier does not accept either of the above cards you can use Dwolla. It is an online payment method for which you just have to pay a fee of $0.25.

PayPal: It can be used for paying the suppliers.

Directories for Finding Suppliers and Wholesalers

You can attend trade shows where you can connect with the major wholesalers and manufacturers belonging to a niche. It enables you to contact suppliers as well as research about the products in one place. This is useful after you have chosen your niche or product. If there is time as well as money at your disposal you can make use of such events to become familiar with the suppliers and manufacturers in the market.

A number of supplier directories are available online which are organized by product, market or niche. Many of them employ a screening process and ensure that genuine suppliers are listed. Mostly they are owned by companies who work for a profit and charge some fees for granting access to the directories. Some of them are Worldwide Brands, SaleHoo, Doba and Wholesale Central.

Frequently Asked Questions

1. Why is it important to find the right supplier?

Finding a suitable supplier happens to be one of the hardest tasks for e-commerce entrepreneurs. The supplier is your most important partner in the drop shipping business model. You have to rely on him for keeping your products in stock, for maintaining the quality of the items, and ensuring that the orders are delivered to the customers in time. A drop shipping business may be ruined in case a wrong choice is made regarding the supplier. So you should not make a decision in haste.

2. How to find a good dropship supplier?

Actually, there are two ways of finding good suppliers for dropshipping. You can manually search online or utilize some wholesale directory such as SaleHoo.

SEARCH ONLINE FOR SUPPLIERS: Type the name of your product and write "supplier" beside it in the Google search bar and see the results. Otherwise you may search on websites such as Aliexpress.com or Alibaba.com. A number of suppliers based in China use these sites for selling their goods.

Use some wholesale directory: You can save time and stay away from e-commerce fraud to a great extent by using a directory. There are more than 8 thousand suppliers who have been screened and verified on SaleHoo. You just need to click a few times and get into touch with some of the authentic suppliers.

Alibaba which is one online resource can be useful for finding and interacting with prospective manufacturers or suppliers. You have to ask questions and find out about their capacity to produce or supply goods and see whether they are appropriate for your enterprise or not.

3. Where can you find the dropship suppliers?

It is possible to find the drop shipping suppliers on shopping sites like Ali-Express, DH-Gate, DX and others. Moreover, they can be found on portals such as Worldwide Brands, DOBA, and Wholesale2B.

4. Where can you get the products for dropshipping?

Besides Ali-Express there are some other e-stores which provide items for selling. They are:

DH-Gate: All the items that are available on Ali-Express can be found here. The only difference is that they are more expensive. For instance, if the price of something is 9 dollars on Ali-Express it might be $11 here. So it is necessary to conduct some research prior to buying things from this site.

Deal-Extreme: its inventory is not very large. But it is suitable for electrical and mechanical goods.

Bang-Good: Instead of being one of the manufacturer's marketplaces it is only one e-commerce store. Therefore the cost of the items is high.

Tom-Top: It is a suitable site for tech items and contains around 1 lakh items.

Chapter 5 Building the website

The next step is to create a website.

Right, with drop shipping we can sell on eBay, Amazon or any other platform we want, but by creating our own website we have our own space within which to attract customers and make them part of our system.

Be clear, it is absolutely possible to create a profitable system without using a proprietary website. We can only sell on other platforms, save a lot of time on the development of the website that we can devote to expanding our catalog, or looking for cheaper suppliers, or any other business.

On the other hand, we lose control of the user experience, of what the customer sees and experiences during the purchase. In general, those who buy one of our products on eBay are not our customers, they are an eBay customer, and eBay will be able to enjoy additional information about this user as the possibility of advertising retargeting to sell similar products in the future.

It is an important decision that should not be underestimated. Finally, let us not forget the potential of these sales platforms (eBay, Amazon) as an advertising channel. You will have already received an item purchased on eBay, inside the box there was a ticket with a discount code for a second purchase, to be made however on the site of the seller.

This is an example of a very clever strategy that allows the company to enjoy the benefits of the eBay platform, but which drives customers to take their site.

My invitation is, therefore, not to necessarily create a website, but not to underestimate its importance, especially on a long-term activity.

Now, let's move on to the more practical aspects of creating a website. We can use many platforms that facilitate development work, based on our skills and the time we intend to dedicate.

One of these that I recommend is Shopify. For a monthly fee that starts at $29 and a percentage of sales (from 2%), Shopify allows us to create an ecommerce within a few days.

We then access to Shopify via the link www.shopify.com and proceed with registration.

The name

The first thing that will be required during registration is the name of the website.

This is a personal choice, but I recommend using an original and imaginative name, which evokes our niche but without being trivial.

For example, for a mountain bike accessory store, it could be a Bikey name, while I would avoid Mountain Bike Accessories because it does not transmit personalities.

One advantage is to have one of the key words in our industry within the name, for example "bike" is contained in "Bikey".

The domain

Along with the choice of the name, it is useful to keep an eye on the web domain. This is the address that will make our online store reachable, so it is essential to have a quality domain.

The domain must absolutely recall the name of our store: according to the example above, we could register www.bikey.com, www.bikey.it and many others.

Unfortunately, we have to deal with availability. In fact, not all the domains we will search for will be available. We can try to add other keywords, for example www.bikeyaccessories.com or www.bikeystore.com, or to change the top-level domain, for example to www.bikey.eu or www.bikey.net.

The possibilities are endless, and the result will be dictated by personal taste. However, I recommend, when possible, to buy a .com domain. If we want to work only in Europe a .eu can do well, and in Italy a .it, but we do not make the mistake of think backwards: if we buy a .it domain, we can sell all over Europe, but we will leave disadvantaged.

For the purchase of a domain, I recommend to directly use the panel of Shopify that allows you to buy it at affordable prices, around $10 / year.

There are providers that would allow us to save a few dollars a year on the domain, but it would be necessary to manually configure DNS entries, a technical issue that is not interesting for the purpose of this book.

Website design

The design of the website is definitely important. The web site graphics must be very clear and the interface simple to navigate.

A well-organized top or side menu is usually a good place to start. Using Shopify, we have available a variety of free themes that can be perfect to start without an investment and with a quality design.

Speech to be done separately for the logo. It can be simple or elaborate, monochromatic or in color, but it is extremely important to have a unique and recognizable logo. Those who are familiar with Photoshop or graphics programs can create it autonomously, otherwise you can get help from freelance designers, for example on Fiverr, starting at $5.

Payment methods

The site is ours, so ours is also the task to commit ourselves to receive payment. The methods are different and at the discretion of the entrepreneur. However, they are now universally accepted methods Pay-Pal and credit cards, through a gateway that can be Braintree or Stripe.

Payment methods such as bank transfer or postal order are optional: it is true that we could get a few more conversions, but managing this type of order is anything but automatic and risks taking too much time compared to the advantage we could expect.

On the other hand, the mark is to be avoided. Since the true sender of the shipment is not us but a third, there is no way to get the payment at the end of the cycle.

Online payments are sometimes subject to fraud, orders paid via stolen or cloned credit cards, fortunately Shopify and Stripe have sophisticated systems to report suspicious orders to us. Finally, in the case of payments with PayPal e-Check it is important to wait until the full amount of the purchase is credited to us before providing the order.

Shopify works well with PayPal and Stripe, which I recommend to use immediately for receiving payments.

Website trust

There are millions of websites, yet a good percentage of people trust only a few of them. Why? It is a problem of credibility, or professionality transmitted.

It is easy for a website to lose its credibility, so we proceed to points with a list of features that our website must necessarily possess in order to be seen as credible and transmit to the user the trust and all the information it needs to buy safely.

- *Service pages.* These can be frequently asked questions (FAQ), contact page, company history, information on payment methods, shipping methods and times, the origin of the objects or the quality of the manufacture.

All the pages that give extra information help to make the buyer understand that there is something else, that we are not just selling products, but that we are dedicated to every single product, that we care about the production chain and materials used. We carefully planned shipping methods to be used and expected the most frequent questions that might arise.

A contact page is absolutely mandatory.

With Shopify, I recommend the free *Help-Center* application for creating help pages and FAQs. Instead, as a contact page, it will be sufficient to use the standard template provided by Shopify.

- *Social pages.* Having a presence on Facebook, Instagram, Twitter is very important to make the buyer understand that he is not alone, that other people in the past have bought from us and found themselves well. We put links to our social profiles at the bottom of our website, and let's take care to have coordinated profile images to give consistency to the brand.

- *Social proof.* It is important to let users know the positive experiences of past buyers, as part of what is called social proof, or social confirmation. The reviews can be for the site in general or for the specific product, but we use the second option only when we have a substantial number of purchases: better not to have the opportunity to review, rather than having it with the item "zero reviews".

Still in the context of social proof, it is also useful to have followers on our pages in social networks. We therefore ask friends and acquaintances to follow us to help us in this adventure.

On Shopify, we can use a very ingenious system to transmit our social proof. An application called *FOMO* allows to show the user small notifications indicating the purchases made on the site in real time. This system, in addition to triggering in his mind the fear of losing the product (FOMO precisely, from Fear of Missing Out), confirms that other people are buying on our site, trusting us and believing in the quality of our products.

The *Ultimate Sales Boost* application has the same goal, but reaches it in a different way: it places a warning that indicates when a product is running out, or that a certain promotion is about to expire, or how many people are looking at the product in the same moment.

These strategies, halfway between social proof and fear of missing out, are extremely effective to push the customer to buy immediately - because postponing the purchase means that, in 90% of cases, this will never be concluded.

- *Trust badges*. These are important brands that our site can show to let the user know that the website is secure and recognized by other companies. We can rely on services like Trust Pilot, Norton Security, McAfee, but also design and apply the logos of our invention, such as an SSL logo or credit card logos accepted.

Of course, we use only logos and brands that have a real relationship with the website: if we do not have a score on Trust Pilot, we cannot put the corresponding badge, an SSL logo will always be valid because the website will use the HTTPS protocol for transactions, but despite being obvious, will give a feeling of security to the less experienced user.

Where to place them? We can have them at the bottom of the pages, in the footer, or near the description of the objects on the product pages.

In this regard, we can find many Shopify applications, including *Trust Seals & Badges*. I recommend trying more than one in order to find the design and positioning that most convinces us.

- *Press*. If we can publish our website, perhaps with a review of the products, on other blogs or magazines, why not take the opportunity to brag about it?

Let's write it clearly. Users who know these magazines will value their opinion and understand that they are facing a serious, professional and not improvised store.

The added value

The topic of added value has already been dealt with previously, and at this point it should already be clear to the reader how they intend to add value to the product sold through the website.

Added value and perceived value actually have the same meaning: this is because in the online purchase, the whole value of the object is purely perceived. Creating added value therefore means simply increasing the value perceived by the user, and this can be done with many different methods.

- Website, photography and high quality graphics. This is fundamental to the credibility of our website. I refer to the design we mentioned earlier, but also to the content of the website.

For example, it is essential to have photos of the product, since the buyer wants to see what he's buying. The photos should be of high quality, on a white background or on real usage scenarios, and if the object has a special packaging, it might help to show this in one of the photos.

Another aspect is the images that you see in the service pages, such as the home page and the company history: these photos must also be of high quality and not too standard, we can also take them on the internet, as long as the license allows us, but let's be original and do not take the same pictures that everyone else is already using!

If possible, we buy some of the items we want to sell. This will allow us to take real, professional or semi-professional photos — excellent photos can now be taken even with a good smartphone, if in ideal environmental conditions.

Finally, we can give these items to our friends and acquaintances to let us leave the first reviews on the website — reinforcing the social proof, as we have seen.

- The contents are very important. If we sell a product, we want its use to be clear. Together with the website, we open a blog dedicated to the sector of which we sell the products, or start a YouTube channel, or create a group on Facebook.

We want to create content that is really useful for fans of the sector, so as to become their point of reference not only for the purchase, but for their absolute hobby. Do we want to sell electronic components?

We can hope that someone will find us autonomously looking for a particular component, or we can write a guide to achieve something, that requires a component that we will sell. It's not hard to guess which method can attract more visitors!

First, I talked about blogs, YouTube and Facebook. This is because we want to show that the community is alive, exists and pulsates around our portal. To become a point of reference in the industry we must not provide one-way information, but be interactive and allow other people who share the same passions to know each other, to confront and help each other. If we can start a process of this kind, we will succeed in having a community that grows autonomously, and that will continue to follow our site and to buy our products. As the activity grows, it will be possible to collaborate with some of these people, asking them to write the articles for the website and, in fact, automating the creation of content!

- Description and technical specifications must be comprehensive. In the creation of the products we are asked for a description. We do not try to dismiss it with a few trivial phrases. Rather, let's get involved and try to be as descriptive as possible. We do not forget information such as weight, dimensions or any type of technical specification can be interesting for the buyer.

So we create the website with images and descriptions of quality, some form of social proof, pages including FAQs, contacts and information on shipping. With the advice we have seen previously, we will be able to get a credible website and will have no problems in being reliable and attractive to customers.

If we use Shopify, we can get help from the many available apps, for example for badges or for connecting to social networks. Let's not forget, however, that the important thing is the result, that you get with Shopify or writing with code all the website, the buyer will see only the final website!

There is therefore no tutorial or specific way to realize our ecommerce. If it meets the basic rules we talked about above, it will be fine. Then we will see later how to get feedback from our customers and how to study their behavior to improve the interface of the site.

Chapter 6 How to Run Your Drop Shipping Company

You have already heard earlier about how you can start your business, but you have no idea about what you should do in order to run it. Studying about how to run your very own drop shipping company can save you some weeks and months of being frustrated.

Things Are Bound to Getting Messy - Since drop shipping is considered convenient, you can expect that it can be confusing as each sale can be complicated especially when other parties are involved. There will be botched orders at times. Some items will be out of stock. You may not be able to fulfil all of the duties you are required to do.

Keep it Simple - You already know that drop shipping is very complicated. You do not have to complicate it further by messing up your system. Make sure that you have created a flawless system that you will follow so that you can track down your inventory and the costs that you have to pay for every time. Instead of choosing some complicated methods, you can choose simpler methods that will do the job well.

Making Things Run Smoothly
The two things that are mentioned above are tips that will help keep you sane while running a drop shipping company. You have to be prepared to run things smoothly depending on the situations that you will encounter. Here are just a few of the possible issues:

- *Your Supplier has Botched an Order*

Even if you already trust your supplier, there will be times when they will make mistakes and you now owning up to the mistake can make things worse. Here are just a few of the things that you can do:

☐ You may want to offer something else to the customer for free in order to make up for the error. It is the best way that you can smooth out the problem.

☐ Apologize to the customer for the mistake. If your customer is not aware that you have a drop shipper, it will only be confusing for the customer. Do not act like an amateur. Admit the mistake and do what you can to pacify the customer.

☐ Allow the supplier to pay for the mistake. Even though you have apologized to the customer for the mistake, it is still not your mistake. If you are dealing with a professional shipping company, they know that they have to pay for the error.

If the supplier where you normally get your items from botch up orders regularly, it is time to search for a new supplier. There are other suppliers who can offer better services than the one you are experiencing.

You have Trouble Managing Your Items

It is only common that you will have some issues with managing your items especially if you have not formulated the right system to follow. If you do a poor job, you may tell some customers that some of your items are available when they are actually out of stock. The constant mistake will turn a lot of customers off. You will lose a lot of customers in the process.

In order to manage your inventory, here are a few things that you can do:

1. Make sure that you have an application that will allow you to keep track of your items easily. We do not live in the Stone Age anymore. You now have a lot of options to make the management of your items easier. Make use of these applications and tools and keeping track of the various items from suppliers will be easier.

2. Have separate files for each supplier. It is only common that you are going to have more than one supplier in order to provide the different items that you need to sell. If you only have one supplier, then you will not have anything to sell if the supplier fails to submit the items you need.

Having more than one supplier can be complicated, though. You may keep track of all the items that you get from one supplier and separate that from the items you get from another supplier. This will allow you to check and see which items are truly out of stock and which ones you still have a lot of.

3. Do not just pick all of the products that suppliers are offering. It may be tempting to pick out all of the cute products that you see. It can also be easy just to choose products that seem to fit your business, but you also have to remember the quality of the items. Are the items worth purchasing? Will people actually pay a lot of money for the items that you are choosing? If you are unsure with which products of picking, choose primary items that are known to sell well.

4. It is okay to pick similar items from different suppliers as long as they look identical. This way, even if the items from one supplier run out, you will have a similar one ready that you can sell to your potential customers.

5. Always coordinate with your sales representative. Your sales representative is here for a reason, and that is to make sure that you will be getting items that will improve your company's name and branding. Always check if the items are available and inform your representative when to start purchasing again, so you will not run out of supplies.

In case even if you have tried your best to manage your stocks you still run out of certain items, tell your customer about it and offer another item that may appease your customer. If the item you are selling appeals to the customer, then you have nothing to worry about. It will even improve your relationship with the customer.

You Have Hired a Bad Vendor

A lot of the items that you are selling will be reliant on your vendor. When a vendor is bad, you will lose time in order to do other things because you will do nothing but follow up the orders of the customers and when they will be shipped. When you have a bad vendor, you can expect that your customers will be irate with you because they were not able to get their items on time. You may even lose customers in the process because they feel like you are wasting their time. At the same time, you know that by hiring the wrong vendor, you are wasting your time and money too.

Not all vendors are good so before you choose a vendor that will be your partner in your business, make sure that you will select a vendor who has already built up a good reputation. To make choosing vendors easier, you can base it on the following:

- *Have criteria that you would like to follow when searching for the right vendor. If one criterion are not achieved by the vendor, then search for another one that can fit your needs better.*
- *Make sure that you will set up a written document wherein your vendor will have to agree with the different terms and conditions that will allow your business to operate smoothly. The document that you are going to create with the help of the lawyer may outline shipping times, inventory updates, order exception resolution among others. This will let you and your vendor know what to do to have a good relationship and work together properly.*
- *If you have more than one vendor, create your very own vendor scorecard, so you will know at the end of the year who among the vendors you are going to keep and who the ones that you will part ways with are. You only need to do what is best for your business.*

When you have a bad vendor, you can cut ties with the vendor unless you have a contract that you have to follow. The moment that you are legally allowed to search for a new vendor do it for the improvement of your drop shipping business.

Dealing with Security and Issues on Fraud

Credit Card Information Storing

If you are going to host your own site, you have to be aware of the following:

- *Get to know the Payment Card Industry (PCI) rules. You have to be aware that this is going to cost a lot of money. There are a lot of compliance rules and audit that you have to be aware of.*
- *In case your client gets his/her account information hacked, it will be your responsibility.*

Knowing that it can be complicated, it is sometimes best if you are only starting your company, that you will not store the credit card information of your clients. You can start venturing into it once your business becomes bigger, but as of now, there are other options that are available that will not make handling your business more complicated than it already is.

Verification System

Since you are only starting out, it is okay to be intimidated with dealing orders and making sure that they are all correct. Remember that you need common sense and caution all the time.

Getting to Know the Address Verification System

In order to prevent fraud, using the Address Verification System will surely help. This requires customers to enter their address connected to their credit card in order to become approved. Through this, credit card thieves will be prevented from making purchases because most of them do not know where the listed addresses are of the credit cards they have stolen. It is already rare for fraud orders to pass through with this system.

It is evident that the order may be considered fraudulent when the billing address and the shipping address are different. If you do not allow items to be released when the billing address and the shipping address is different, however, you will lose sales if you would not allow this to occur so what the signs that you should watch out for in order to know if the order is fraudulent or not are?

- *The names are different - The names may be different because of two possible reasons. The first reason is that the order is fraudulent while the second reason is that the purchase is a gift.*
- *E-mail addresses do not seem authentic - It is very easy to create a free e-mail address but normally, people who use their e-mail address will incorporate a part of their name into it. If you see e-mail addresses that make no sense, this may be a sign of fraud.*
- *Most expensive shipping - Since a lot of fraudsters are paying with another person's credit card; they do not care if they pick the most expensive way to ship. Of course, this can also mean that they would like to get the items that they ordered immediately.*

So what should you do if you suspect that an order is a fraud? This is the time when you should make good use of your phone. Remember that since a lot of people would not like to put their real numbers on their order, you will either get a false number or you can get the number where you can talk to the person who ordered, so everything will be cleared. Honestly, this is easy to do in the beginning when you are not getting enough orders yet but can be more complicated and harder to monitor when you are handling a lot of orders at the same time.

Chargeback's

Do you understand what chargeback is? Basically, this is when a customer contacts his/her credit card company to complain about a charge that your company has made. The amount will temporarily be taken from your account, and you have to prove that you were able to provide the services or items to the customer who has complained of getting charged. It is okay if you can find proof but if you don't, there will be a processing fee charged to your account. The worst thing that can happen is you will not be given the privilege of having a merchant account anymore.

There are different reasons for getting chargebacks:

- Fraud

- *The customer forgot about ordering*
- *The customer did not like the item or service received.*

When you receive a chargeback, it is not the proper time to contemplate about what have gone wrong. You barely have time to do anything so make sure that you will do your best to answer as quickly as you can.

To Get Your Money Back

You have been charged a certain fee because of the chargeback, and your main goal is to get your money back. How are you going to do that? Remember to provide documentation which proves that you have delivered the items ordered from you. If the transaction is legitimate, your chances of getting your money back are certain.

To Win the Issue

You need the billing and the shipping address on the card information details to be the same. If the details are not the same, your chances of getting a charge back lessen.

Dealing with Returns

It may be easy to start making your own return policy without realizing how other suppliers do it. You have to understand the policy of each supplier that you have. It will make dealing with things easier. For example, they may have a 60 day return policy. When this occurs, you can be generous with your return policy as well. Of course, if you have more than one supplier, you have to consider all so even if there is one that offers 60 day return policy, if the other one only offers 45 day return policy, you need to adjust your terms.

How Customers Return Items

This is the process followed by customers whenever they need to return items:

1. A customer requests to return the item/s received.
2. You talk to your supplier about getting a Return Merchandise Authorization.
3. The customer mails the item back to the supplier and not to you. Take note of this. The RMA# should be specified.
4. The supplier refunds the amount.
5. You return the funds to your customer in full amount.

The process seems to be easy right? Yet, if you have tried returning an item that you do not like in the past, you know that there are different things that can complicate the return process.

Defective Items

When it comes to defective items, you are risking your business because people might not want to order from you again because you are selling something that does not work. Another bad thing about this is that you would have to pay for shipping. Unfortunately, you cannot pass on this fee to anyone else.

If the item is inexpensive, it may be a better option to let the customer keep the old item and just ship a new one, but if it is expensive, then you may have to ask the customer to return it while you handle the shipping fees.

Here are some of the advantages that can be received if the items are simply exchanged without the need for the defective items to be shipped back:

- *It is more cost effective - It may not be worth it to spend a lot of money on shipping the defective item back to you if the shipping is worth the actual cost of the item.*
- *You will score major points with the client - It is very rare that companies will allow clients not to return the old item anymore so if you do this, you can expect that your clients will be blown away and would be more trusting when it comes to dealing with you.*
- *You may talk your supplier into handling the shipping costs of the new items that will be sent to the client. This will depend on your relationship with your supplier, though.*

A lot of companies usually require the buyers to handle the shipping fee of returning various items that they have ordered, even if the item is defective. In order to stand out, you can order free shipping. You can expect that customers will take note of this.

A Few Possible Issues with Shipping Rates

When it comes to shipping rates, it can be very complicated if you have more than one supplier. Once again, you need to adjust your rates depending on the costs. To make the rates more uniform and less complicated, here are some ideas:

- *Type Rates - This means that you are going to have rates depending on the type of items that are being ordered by the client.*
- *Flat Rate - This may be the easiest one. There will be a standard flat rate that will be followed no matter what the items that are ordered are.*
- *Real Time Rates - You will have to compute the real amount of shipping based on the items that are ordered and the client's location. It can be complicated especially if the items that are ordered by the client comes from different warehouses.*

It is common for merchants sometimes to spend weeks contemplating on the rules that they have to make regarding shipping. One advice is this: implement a shipping policy that makes sense especially when the whole shipping expedition is considered. Since you are just starting out, take it slow. You will be formulating shipping policies that will make more sense in the future.

Shipping Internationally

Even though shipping internationally has changed drastically over the past years, it may still have some issues as compared to local shipping. If you want to ship internationally, here are just a few things that you have to consider:

- *Additional charges from suppliers because most of them will have different rates when processing international orders.*
- *Higher shipping fees that may result in some problematic orders.*
- *There will be excessive costs especially if you have to ship items that are heavy.*
- *There are different limitations that should be considered depending on the country that you are going to ship to.*

It will be up to you to decide if shipping internationally is actually worth it. It is not recommended when you are just starting out. You are always better off offering your business to local clients first. Who knows, probably in the future, you can offer to ship internationally.

Fulfilling the Order of Clients

It has already been discussed earlier that it is best to have more than one supplier as it allows you to ensure that all items will be in stock whenever people order but choosing the right suppliers that will help you run your company should be done with careful consideration. Some of the things that you should do are the following:

Choose suppliers based on location - It will still be easier if you would choose suppliers that will not have a hard time getting the products that you have ordered all the time. This means that if you have some customers that are within their route, you may choose them because of this reason alone.

Choose suppliers based on the items that they have available - You cannot force suppliers to have items in stock when they don't.

Choose suppliers based on price - It will be a nice idea if you can choose suppliers based on how they price their items but realistically, this is not possible because it will be complicated to figure out which supplier offers the best price.

Remember that as your business grows, the goal of suppliers is to give you the best items that you need. They will bid based on what your requirements are and usually, the one that bids the lowest will be chosen.

Picking the Carrier to Ship Items

The right carrier that can do the shipping for you will make a lot of difference with your business. Here are some carriers that you can consider:

1. US Postal Service - This may be the best carrier to choose if you are only shipping small items and if you are shipping internationally.

2. UPS/FedEx - They are well known for shipping large and heavy products locally, so you will not have any problems with hiring them for shipping large items.

Remember that when you are still creating options regarding your shipping, make sure that you will specify how long it will take before the products are sent. Choose the best choice for each order.

Chapter 7 The Dropshipping Model of Business

Drop shipping is an e-commerce model which involves online business. It came into vogue in the year 2006. The e-commerce stores of China were launched that year in the United States and Ali-Express got recognition. Few businessmen set up their own stores for making profits. They decided to use Ali-Express because it was less expensive for them. Other people also followed in their footsteps and drop shipping developed into a well-known form of business.

At present, it is one of the most rewarding forms of business which may be established with negligible or zero investment. Wayfair and Zappos are some well-known examples of enterprises which have adopted the drop shipping form of business.

New entrepreneurs, usually the Gen Zers and the Millennials use this model. They delegate the work of packing and shipping the goods to the suppliers this helps to decrease operational costs and gives them more time for marketing and customer acquisition.

What is a Dropshipping Business

Drop shipping is a form of enterprise in which you do not need to own an inventory, maintain a warehouse or store goods. **Moreover, you do not even have to ship the items to your customers.**
A supply chain has to be managed in this model of business. The retailer does not own an inventory. He just focuses on promoting the goods and marketing his supplier's goods. In turn, he earns a decent profit.

As a drop-shipper the retailer acts as an intermediary between the buyers and suppliers. He receives an order from the customer and passes it on to the supplier. He keeps a certain amount of the money paid by the customer as a commission for himself. The supplier dispatches the items from his warehouse to a particular customer.

One new trend which is gaining popularity in this field of business is private label type of dropshipping. In this, the retailer requests the manufacturer to produce some customized items and dropship them on his behalf. Apparel with customized logos, simple keepsakes, custom made nutritional products, and pictures are some examples of such items.

How do You Make Money with Dropshipping

Actually, in this form of business, the goods are sold at a higher price by the drop-shipper to earn profits. For instance, he might sell an item for $300 or $350 while its wholesale price may be just $250. In this way, he can earn $50 or $100 as commission. He arbitrages the goods for profits.

> Although the profit margins in this type of business are between 15-45% on a general basis, luxury goods, jewelry and durable items like electronics may yield 100% profit margins. **The key lies in selecting the right niche or product, finding the right supplier for the product, and entering a market that is not already saturated with that item.**

If you want to gain a higher profit margin you can use the services of the manufacturer for supplying the goods to the customer directly instead of relying on a vendor or supplier. Eliminating the middleman's role in the supply chain may improve the profit margin. But all the manufacturers do not provide drop shipping services.

In spite of some drawbacks once the drop shipping enterprise gets established and gains momentum it can become one money minting mechanism that does not need much input. Irwin Dominguez's drop shipping enterprise is a remarkable example of a business that earned USD 1 million in just eight months. It provides an affirmation for the fact that there is a lot of latent potential in this business.

Where do You Keep inventory

Drop shipping is a type of business in which the retailer carries on the business with no inventory. He buys things only after selling them; he does not store anything with him. The inventory is kept in the warehouses of the suppliers who fulfill the orders for the retailer. The stocks of goods are maintained by the suppliers.

The Unique Features of this Model

- The drop-shipper can set prices on his own.
- He can sell the products without partnering with some manufacturer. He can utilize platforms like eBay, Amazon or Ali-Express for this.
- The drop-shipper gains profits by arbitraging the products.

Gary V., Wine Library TV & Vayner Media Founder has rightly said, "There has never been a better time, in the history of time, than right now to start a business."

Chapter 8 Shopify Dropshipping

Shopify is a cloud-based and cloud-hosted online commercial platform which helps you manage and grow your business after you have started it. The best part is that you can start your business through Shopify from anywhere you want, provided you have a decent internet connection. Shopify lets you explore its facilities for a trial period of 14 days and later on, you need to have a subscription to get started with your business. There are three packages at three different price ranges that you can choose from depending upon the structure and size of your business. During your trial period, you can use the features of Shopify as much as you want without a credit card and at the same time make sales. You will notice Shopify allows you to manage inventory, products, and track your payments and shipping. In short, it is your manager and helps you to transition into the drop shipping industry. Also, accessing this platform does not require you to be proficient in design or be a developer yourself; you can easily teach yourself with help available online and by exploring its simple, user-friendly interface. As you can use Shopify from anywhere, you will find that you can use a variety of languages when sending emails, blogging, or dealing with checking out for the convenience of the customers. Currently, the available languages are English, Brazilian Portuguese, Danish, Dutch, Finnish, French, German, Hindi, Italian, Japanese, Korean, Malay, Norwegian, Simplified Chinese, Spanish, Swedish, Thai, and Traditional Chinese. Additionally, you need to have your domain set up according to your requirements and it is always advised to use a customized domain name. You should be ready to open a merchant account when you are setting up your store. After the customers have made their payments, the revenue is deposited in this account. Hence, you earn through this very account after you have fulfilled your shipping orders. You can easily accept online payments through third parties, who are known as payment providers. As drop shipping through Shopify lets you sell globally and locally, you can accept payments in multiple currencies. The types of currencies you have access to mainly depends on the third-party payment gateways or processors you have chosen to use. You are free to sell on multiple platforms that include social media, mobile, web, and online marketplaces. To start, you should simply see where this trial period takes you. All this information is widely available through various online resources thus, you should not worry at all!

How do you build a Shopify Dropshipping website?

Creating a Shopify account

This should be a very familiar step if you are comfortable with using the internet and social media. During this process, you will need a store name, so it is much better to have brainstormed ideas beforehand in order to have a catchy name. This name helps you set your store apart from your competitors and reflects on the products that you are looking to sell. You will need to register an account with Shopify and click the tab called "Get Started" - this is where you begin the process on their website. As you move along, you will get questions on this website so that they can compile information about your drop shipping history. Go ahead and fill them out. You will be given questions about your physical address followed by your email address. After you are done with these, the website will automatically take you to the backend of your store. Expect an official email from Shopify that has your store's URL in it. They will provide you with a URL in the email that will look like this: Your-Store-Name.myshopify.com/admin.

After the sign-up process, this is where the real work begins. You are introduced to the various features that Shopify offers and how can they be utilized for your store and business. You will be taken to your dashboard on Shopify and be provided with a lot of tasks, and based on your priorities and time you have, you can start working on them one by one. The most important ones are setting up your domain and designing and adding products to your store. Hence, it is suggested that you focus on these steps first.

Adding products to your store

Your store displays the products you want your customers to purchase, and your product line shows what your niche and vision is. If you have jotted down some ideas about what sort of products you want to have this could be an exciting way for you to get started. This part does not take that much time and hence, is most convenient for you to start with. You will notice that with just a few mouse clicks, you will be able to set up the items you want to display on your online storefront and seamlessly move the items around if needed. This helps in the long run when you are only focusing on designing your store. When you have an idea about the type of products your store will display, it is easier to build the themes and design the look. This saves you time and energy.

Oberlo is the default drop shipping application set by Shopify for entrepreneurs who are just starting their drop shipping business. In your account, when you go to the "Products" menu you will be able to locate the tab "Find more products to sell". This automatically lets you navigate through the Oberlo app. It is an application that helps you upload products directly to your Shopify store. You have access to a whole array of preset products in the app; you can find anything from toys to clothes within various prices ranges. It helps you learn your way around the app, lets you explore its library, and allows you to dropship the products directly on the doorstep of your customers. It doesn't get easier than this. Although you have to add products manually to your Shopify store, it is just a matter of a few mouse clicks. The application is user-friendly and allows you to import products directly from the Oberlo marketplace and Ali-Express. You do not need to worry about fulfilling your customers' orders nor do you have to think of going on a hunt for new or better suppliers. You can also write your own product descriptions, choose photos of the products, and much more. You will find their pricing of products on the app as well and can choose according to whatever your budget is. Overall, you have a manager through Oberlo that takes care of everything for you.

To add new products, you need to select "Products" which you should find on the left side of the screen, and then click "More actions" and "Find more products to sell" consecutively. The interface is very easy to use and you can use the search bar to look for items that you want to add to your store. Try to be specific and use the right keywords to get the best search results. You are free to add items which you prefer to your store by choosing "Select Product". You will see that there are certain costs mentioned on the product page. These include the pricing field where you are required to put your retail price along with shipping and supply costs. After all these steps, you should click "Add Product", and your Shopify store will have these items added by Oberlo. For each product, all you need to do is repeat these steps.

Editing details of the product

The products you are choosing for your store come with product descriptions with specific keywords. These words would be either similar or very different to what you were initially looking to use for your products. In cases like this, do not hesitate to make edits wherever necessary. This will require a bit of time and you need to put in the effort to ensure that the names and descriptions of products displayed on your store are relevant and significant to the niche of your store. It is better to personalize these to make them more lucrative when the customers pay your store a visit. You need to have knowledge of what types of keywords work for what type of products. Apart from the right keywords, tags could be of great use as they can directly link to the collections and categories that your store is divided into. These labels help to make your store more efficient for searching and promotes ease of navigation for the customers.

Setting up a collection

According to your product line, you can further sub-categorize your products. You can do it according to your convenience or according to the market of your niche. Usually, you will notice that drop shipping stores set their collections up under various categories, which include items on sales, color and so on. This does not only help you to keep track of the order list and update the inventory but also makes things much more comfortable for your customers when they explore your product line. When you divide the types of items you offer under designated categories, searching becomes quicker and helps save customers time. It allows them ease of browsing and can be an important factor in turning them into returning customers.

To add or create a collection, you need to go to "Products" in the navigation on the left-hand side and click on "Collections". Then, click on "Create Collection" which will directly take you to a page where you can name your collection and add a description. The interesting part is that these collections do not have to be put in manually, they can easily be added automatically using filters too. Both types of collections can be used to your advantage but creating a manual collection is certainly more time consuming and contains only the products that you have chosen individually. With a manual collection, as you are working on this from scratch, until and unless you make an addition or remove a product, your line will display the products that you added. For smaller catalogs, putting this much effort in is worth it but for larger ones, this is not the most practical way. On the other hand, you can use filters and change settings when you create an automatic collection, which can help you create collections of items that are on sale, for example, but at a much faster rate than doing it manually, one by one.

Setting up your store

To set up your store, you need to click "Online Store" located on the sidebar on the left-hand side of the Shopify backend. Here you will be able to explore different themes, among which many of them are free Shopify themes. You can look into their theme marketplace as well and customize wherever necessary. You need to set up and design your store after you are done sorting through all the products. It is easier to transition into this step after you are aware of what you are offering as it helps you pick relevant themes accordingly.

If you want to customize and not settle for the themes already available on the site, you can choose the "Customize" option after you are done selecting a theme. You are allowed to make edits to the theme that represents your store's identity. There should be a toolbar on the left-hand side inside your theme builder. You can get started customizing according to your preferences from this step onwards. You can work with colors, social media, the checkout page, typography, and many other things when you are setting up your store. It is better to do trial runs when choosing a theme and play around with colors. When you have different versions, it becomes easier to make comparisons before making a final decision. Moreover, this customization also can also allow you to use images, which is the easiest way to connect with first time consumers.

Adding a variety of pages
Along with various types of themed content, Shopify also allows you to add pages about your business. Click the tab called "Pages" found on the left-hand side of the page and following this, you should click "Add Page". The variety of pages include an About page, a Contact page, Shipping & Returns and FAQ. The information on these pages makes it easy for customers to figure out any query they may have. Technical answers can be found on these pages and customers can find answers to their queries easily. It also gives customers a chance to look through the design and theme of your store. If you are comfortable with SEO (Search Engine Optimization), you can easily make modifications to the title, description, and URL in order to help specify what you would want your clients to see when they use the search engine to look for your store.

Setting up navigation

Navigating through a website helps you to understand the entire layout of the website along with explore various kinds of information on the website. The preset settings in navigation gives the customers the first impression of your store. These settings allow you to choose which pages or collections will appear on your 'Menu' tab according to your preferences. You need to specify and strategize how you would want your store to be perceived when clients pay a visit. You can put up an About page that allows your customers to quickly gain insight about your business and can attract them to your niche and vision. Many Shopify drop-shippers choose to upload their collections on their webpage to showcase the best of what the store has to offer. It completely depends on what you want your customer to see at first glance. Once you have that in mind, you can strategize accordingly. You should take time to decide which pages or collections you want to put up on the menu.

You should have already set up all of your collections, products, and pages before you begin making changes to your navigation. Now, you should go to the menu of your backend and on the left-hand side, you will find "Navigation" which lets you add any item you want. You will be able to add a link, a page, or even an entire collection. On the menu page, you need to click "Add menu item" and name your item. After you do this, you will see the "Link" tab where you can select any item that you find relevant from the entire list of collections, pages, and products that you have already set up. To add any particular category or collection, go on "Collections" and make a selection according to your preference. A similar method is followed if you want to add another page. If you want your menu to include the About page of your store, select "Pages" and then click the About page.

Editing the general preferences of the site

The title of your site along with the meta description can both be edited or completely changed depending on how you want it on the Shopify backend. If you are too hesitant to go out there and make choices, remember that there is always an option to make changes later on. You will find the "Preferences" tab on the left-hand side of the menu where you can make any changes you think would be necessary. Facebook Pixel and Google Analytics can be added to this section as well.

Setting up a domain

You may think that not having a custom name will not impact the performance of your business. To understand this from a technical perspective, it is possible for your store to work perfectly without having a custom URL, but you cannot deny the underlying benefits having a custom name will bring. Firstly, it gives your business a professional image and secondly, it attracts customers faster overall as it has the potential to give your store more visibility. If you do not consider adding a domain name, the default URL will be **https://YOUR-STORE-NAME.myshopify.com/** which is not easy to remember and read when you see it for the first time. You need to think from the customer's point of view and find ways that will help them understand your store's niche and appeal more clearly.

On the backend of Shopify, you will find the tab "Online Store" on the left-hand side. This is where you can find your domain, and connect, transfer, and buy a domain, whichever applies to your case. There are many domain providers such as Host-Gator and Blue-host, that help you obtain a domain. If you have an existing one, you can easily connect it with your Shopify. In a case where you do not have a domain through a third party, you can contact these providers. The prices for a custom domain have an estimated starting price of around 11 dollars for a yearly domain. If you have a domain already, the system can automatically link your domain name to your Shopify store. On the other hand, you are allowed to pay, manage, and renew your domain directly from the backend of Shopify. However, policies between your domain provider and Shopify may vary so it is much safer to have gone through both of their guidelines before making any calls.

Setting up payments

After you are done setting everything up, you need to understand how the payment system works. Just like the other steps, it is simple and easy to understand. You will find "Settings" on the menu on your left. Click "Payment Providers". You are allowed to make changes in the settings where you can state your preferred method of payment. There are some default settings which allow you to use Shopify Payments to make transactions. PayPal, on the other hand, contacts you through email after your first sale is made and gives you instructions on setting up a PayPal Merchant account. You should have sound knowledge in this area and choose secured payment methods to avoid mishandling and mismanagement.

Exploring other Shopify Drop shipping applications

The Shopify app store has a lot to offer and you should not settle before you have explored each of them briefly. As mentioned earlier, Oberlo is the default drop shipping app on Shopify but there are many others which you can subscribe to for dropshipping. Make sure you add ones that are relevant and most convenient for your product line. It is suggested that you compare these applications available on Shopify before getting a fully paid package.

Spread-App

The Spread App allows you to add hundreds of thousands of products to your store and gives you the flexibility to create customized product descriptions for your site. You can also display products from Amazon on your Shopify store. This means your customers can click on any product link and make a purchase directly from Amazon. It charges around five dollars per month, which is extremely affordable, even for a small business. Their services allow you to get automatic updates on pricing and inventory. It follows a very simple method where all you need to do is put the URL of the Amazon product on the Spread dashboard which then pulls the product using your Amazon API.

Selecting a paid a payment plan for your Shopify Dropshipping store

Investing in a good paid plan for your store is necessary for you to reap all the benefits of this user-friendly application. Of course, there is a plan available for free, which should be how you get familiar with Shopify but you should not rely on the trial version if you want to have long term growth. This trial period is 14 days; you should look into price packages according to your budget during these 2 weeks or well before them. You need to keep in mind that within the trial period, you will not be able to sell anything, hence, purchasing a paid monthly plan is mandatory to earn through Shopify. On the bottom of your dashboard, you will see "Select a Plan". All you need to fill in your credit card details after you have chosen a package and that's it! Now you can start earning!

Chapter 9 How to Dropship on Amazon and eBay

Dropshipping On Amazon

Dropshipping with Amazon is great and it is just another good service provider to sell products with. Selecting a service provider like Amazon will also include FBA and also FBA Fulfillment. When a Dropshipping company decides to go with Amazon for its product distribution it will open a few doors. First of all, Amazon handles all of the shipping and handling that goes into delivering the product. Amazon is going to pack and weigh all of the items and record all metrics into their system for data tracking.

The company will need to purchase electronic product storage space and also the time amount that they want the shop to be running on the internet. The space to sell will be paid for as long as the company keeps getting consistent sales with the product line. FBA will fulfill all of the needs that the customer has with FBA fulfillment. With this set in place, selling times and schedules can be optimized in many ways to handle recurring transactions and even personalized PO's from company to company. FBA fulfillment is going to keep track of all clients that buying on a routine basis by organizing their needs and the Drop shipping schedules that have been made to fulfill.

Amazon weighs the product per pound. These rates apply to any of the products shipped so there can be a good spending system at play for moving different varieties of the product value. As Amazon states, "Make sure the products are e-commerce ready."

This means that the company must make sure that the products they are going to be selling are practically already online and they are in a queue that is going to sell fast. One of the cool things is that Amazon will let you ship your products to them and the company can begin selling their company-branded items that are going to be great marketing for the company

Amazon also provides customer support for all of the customers and orders that are placed with the company. If there is anything that goes wrong with the package during shipment Amazon will contact both the buyer and the seller to keep full awareness of what is going on. This is a great play because most people know the name Amazon and they trust this name. It is important to stand with a trusted company if the company at hand has no name for itself. Although a few followers on the social accounts is great and shows effort it makes it all the much easier to dropship having a multimillion dollar company backing you up with professional labeling and a reputation that keep the company grounded.

Dropshipping on e-Bay

Drop shipping with eBay works the same way as with Amazon but there are different benefits like having bidding structures. These selling techniques can welcome new sellers that have different product value and are looking for rare items. They use the same time of hosting platform. The business owner just purchases inventory space but there must be a good part on the seller if there is going to be a custom product sold. Drop-shippers communicate with many distributors and this is how they can supply such a diverse market.

Chapter 10 What to do next?

We know how to create a system that can capture visitors, turn them into customers and let them receive the product. And it is extraordinary to think that all this can work without our daily work:

- The customer comes from advertising campaigns, online research, marketing emails we designed.

- The order is made by the customer independently. Shopify makes it easy to purchase, PayPal and Stripe can receive money without manual intervention and get them directly to our account.

- The order is automatically forwarded to the supplier or warehouse.

- The package is prepared and sent directly to the customer who purchased it.

What's left to do? Optimize the process!

Every aspect described in this book can be deepened with dozens of other readings and dedicated courses.

We can therefore dedicate ourselves to improving advertising on Facebook and Google to reduce the cost of visits, improve the website to increase the conversion rate, work on email marketing to get repeat purchases and better feedback.

Once we reach a good level, we can *scale* the company. What does it mean?

Consider having a budget of $ 50 a day, which takes us on average 200 visits and 4 purchases. Since we do not have to worry about the infrastructure of the website, the shipments, the stock, what would happen if we double the advertising budget?

We could expect to receive double the visits, and then sell double the products.

In a real situation there are several variables, we could find that the cost per click increases if we increase the budget, thus allowing us to sell more but with a lower margin for each sale. On the contrary, the cost of the products could decrease with the increase of the volume of business, thanks to better agreements that we can get with the sellers.

A guide on how to scale business is beyond the scope of this book, but I would like to reflect on how drop shipping is a highly scalable system, because with increasing orders, our volume of work will not increase, but only the figures we will see on the screen — at the exit but also at the entrance!

The most important thing is to act, not be afraid to start a business, if well studied and planned, and especially if you are ready to learn what you need to bring it to success.

An ecommerce store structured with drop shipping can bring very interesting economic income, which can reach and even exceed a very high average salary.

All this does not come without effort: of course, we do not have to build a shop in cement and bricks, but we must learn to understand the functioning of every single component of our business, optimize, test and optimize again.

I hope this book may have given you an idea on how to start your business online using a completely automatic, flexible and without initial investment.

To improve, day after day, I still advise to deepen the topics such as web marketing, the development of ads on social media, the most effective email marketing techniques and the creation of sales funnel.

Chapter 11 Taking a Look at Current Trends

In case you are new to 2019, we need to talk about current trends and how they affect your business. You see, there are many different trends that gain popularity each year, which means they are booming in business. Knowing what these trends are and how they may work for you is a great way to push your drop shipping business to the stars.

Trends become popular and they are passed through word of mouth. Suddenly you're seeing ads for them everywhere and everyone is talking about it. An easy example could be the Pumpkin Spice Latte or avocado on toast. You don't know when it started, but these fads often already existed they are just in the spotlight.

If your niche fits you should be ready to capitalize on any current trends, and also be aware of them. This can truly make a difference in how well your business works. Just because you don't care about a trend doesn't mean it can't care for you; meaning, that doesn't mean you can't still make money off of it.

Knowing your consumers and understanding their needs is a great step toward creating a strong business model.

When trends emerge they usually do so suddenly, in an explosion that often takes everyone by surprise. That's part of the fun of following a trend. Of course, some of them are long-lasting and have been around for a while as well, so it's up to you to discern what to put your time and money into.

Now that consumers have more access to information through the internet and their smartphones, it's more important than ever to get on board with what they are interested in. This means that they can not only learn more about these things but then find and purchase them faster. Impulse buying is a huge part of sales these days.

Hopping on the bandwagon is a great way to lure people to your drop shipping business as well. If they see a product they've been hearing a lot about on their site it draws them to you. They could end up purchasing more from you, or using you as their go-to site if you treat them well. That's why it's important to have a smooth-running operation from start to finish.

Having access to this type of information means now more than ever you need to be active in your online role and pushing for those sales. It's so easy for consumers to find more about the products they desire or find places to order them cheaply. You want to be on their radar, and this means being informed about what they want.

Now that you have an idea about why trends are so important when it comes to your business and your marketability, we can go a bit more in-depth. Let's learn about a few of the trends that are relevant today and why they might be worth a second look.

Hopefully, you will find a few things that you can incorporate into your own business.

Current Consumer Online Purchase Trends Worth A Look:

Keeping yourself up to date on current consumer online purchase trends is a necessary part of your job if you want to find success with your drop shipping business. Picking up on a purchasing trend soon enough can increase your profits by a high margin.

Let's go in-depth and explore a few of those popular trends that are current moneymakers.

Health and Wellness

One of the biggest trends out there right now is health and wellness. This trend has been slowly percolating through the years, and now here we are, where it is one of the most thriving trends of 2019.

When we talk about health and wellness we mean more than just eating right and exercising. Wellness has expanded to mean so much more, including mental and spiritual wellness as well as physical. This can translate to eating more conscientiously, taking supplements, essential oils, meditation, yoga, and more.

The rise of fitness trackers has been picking up through the years as well, and people even track the foods they eat or the times they sleep, because now more than ever it is important to look after their health.

Consumers aren't looking to work too hard though, they easily jump to the next fad in the hopes it gives the results that they desire.

More than that, now consumers care about the ethics of the products they consume. So many brands have started preached cruelty-free products or ethically sourced material. This translates to a broader image of presenting complete transparency.

Health and wellness products involve more than just vitamins, they can also include organic products, smartwatches, and even the clothing that is worn.

Wanting to be "well" in all aspects of their lives leads to a desire to purchase a specific niche of items that fit into their ideals. This can include all basic products and beyond, so it's a great way to add it into your store if the desire strikes you.

As an example, going vegan has become ever more popular these days and is touted as being rejuvenating and a better option environmentally as well. There are also more and more products being manufactured that can be considered "green" and healthy for the environment, from how they are made to the resources used to create them.

Realizing that there is a whole customer base out there which cares about these things means there is a huge market available to create a business plan on.

Healthy eating is important and so is organic sourcing, but even the idea of "treating yourself" and working on taking care of your mental health has pushed all sorts of products out there. Bath bombs have taken off in recent years, and the more creative companies have made quite a tidy profit on selling them as a great treatment for self-care.

Self-care in itself is a huge industry as people flock more and more to the idea that it is important to take time to enjoy for themselves or even just look after their bodies more. That is where there are hundreds of thousands of products in this market targeted toward just that niche. Starting to get a few ideas?

Being a brand that is seen as progressive is a great way to build your audience and appeal to a wide range of people. Almost no one is going to sit around and say, "Oh no, they are environmentally conscious, I don't want to shop there."

When you're choosing the niche you hope to establish, you need to consider trends like this because there may be ways to fit it into what you are selling, or maybe it already naturally relates to it. Either way, be smart about it because health and wellness care aren't going away any time soon. People want to feel good and they want to feel good about themselves, and this is where that trend directs them.

Ethical Use of Artificial Intelligence (AI)

Looking at this section you are probably feeling a little confused, what does artifical Intelligence have to do with consumer trends? This is a big conversation starter these days is Artificial Intelligence grows more and more advanced and more and more businesses start using them.

AI and digital marketing now consistently work together, because it is honestly just easier to let the AI collect and analyze data. There are often common issues and ethical debates that arise when it comes to using Artificial Intelligence in regards to consumers.

Obviously utilizing AI can mean a better customer experience overall, because it can help curate content for that customer to keep them interested. The problem is, of course, when that Artificial Intelligence is considered to overstep the ethical bounds.

There was a whole newsworthy saga recently concerning the creator of Facebook and how their ads targeted, etc. Consumers are wary when it comes to AI because they believe their privacy is important, and it most definitely is.

Using AI doesn't need to be an ethical quandary as long as those who use it are transparent concerning it. AI can be of great use to any business especially when using it to amass and understand data.

What could be a long and arduous process for a person can take minutes and an algorithm for Artificial Intelligence? The issue is making sure it is used ethically, and the debate is about what those standards truly entail.

Utilizing AI is important, and so it making sure that they provide fair and unbiased results. Too easily it can be spotted that Artificial Intelligence is still taking up our natural inclinations toward bias. Amazon recently had to correct their hiring algorithm because it was unfair toward women. Insane that even AI has that issue, right?

Consumers don't mind brands using AI they just want to know that it is being used rightfully and ethically. If consumers don't believe that's happening then they consistently want the government to come to make a decision in regards to the businesses, which is a huge difference from when the tech boom began.

There are plenty of ways to check through your AIs or algorithms and make sure they are following suit with this consumer trend. It's your duty as the business owner and brand to make sure they comply with what your consumers desire. By doing so, and being transparent about it, you are opening doors for your customer base to feel a sense of trust and partnership with you that others might not.

Confused on how to go about this? Don't worry, IBM created a package that can help target any bias or issues within such algorithms, and you can use it to really in-depth examine the tools you use. Then you can start working on corrections.

Really, it's not too hard to be aware of the trends that are out there, especially this one, because you already are consuming products and are a part of platforms that are working diligently to eradicate problems in the ethics of AI usage.

So don't stress. It can feel like a lot when all these consumer trends seem targeted at holding businesses accountable, but now that you know what is important to your base you can start early. Use this knowledge to your advantage before you even open your doors to sales, and can't go wrong.

Legislative Brands

More and more consumers believe that businesses and brands need to be striving toward having a positive impact on the world and those they serve. This is not necessarily a bad thing, but its definitely making it a bit more complicated.

Going back to the idea of health and wellness, this is quite similar, as people push for ethical practices and consumerism.

Having a legislative brand means companies and businesses are using their power to push for legislation. That's right, our favorite brands want to promote their businesses by becoming a part of the changes that take place in our government and day to day life.

Imposing a positive impact is a great mindset, but there needs to be a lot of consideration when it comes to having those who thrive off of consumers money forcing legislation. Whose interests are being touted here? At least, that's how consumers used to feel when it came to this type of lobbying.

Now it is often expected for brands to push toward constructive changes that are better for everyone, at least, that's how it is being sold. The trend is for those who can make changes do so, and do good.

Instead of wanting companies to stay out of it, consumers expect brands to push for social changes and more. They want the brands to have commentary and dialogue concerning the politics of today, and that is a huge shift from just a few decades ago.

This type of branding for your company can be a positive and negative thing. Pushing for a plan that stands up to what you believe is right, or even just politically correct, can alienate you from a large customer base even as it collects you an audience. We see it all the time on social media and in the news because it is a huge conversation starter.

Choosing to implement a plan like this is something most brands think heavily about. It matters what your passions are, what your niche is, and if you can stand to be picky about who chooses your products. This is a trend that is more advisable for once your business is on its feet and you can afford to take chances.

An entire business model needs to be made in advance of this type of action, and unless that's your sole claim to fame there need to be serious safeguards in place.

It's more than just about appearing a certain way as well, you have to be ready to be authentic and listen to the voices of the people you are trying to speak for. This can be hard for many brands, and inauthenticity will ring hollow if you aren't following the so-called "rules" of the movements.

If this is a route that interests you, there do not need to be huge changes and promotions. Some things as simple as taking a stand on sexual harassment in the workplace, or providing more breaks and time off for your employees can show you care about what people are saying. Being a brand that cares can do wonders for your image, and also give you the chance to be a part of the changes that are being pushed for.

This trend is a positive one that you could choose to take part in easily. A few steps go a long way toward making a difference, and there's not really anything to dislike about becoming a legislative style brand, as long as you can handle any potential fallout.

Open-Source

At first, open-source can seem like a bit of a backfire. Putting out all your ideas and innovations out in the open so that anyone can take advantage of them? But that's all your hard work, isn't it? You worked on it and you deserve to reap the rewards.

Think of it this way though, now you personally have the opportunity to find ideas and solutions due to open-sourcing that you might now have been able to discover or afford to research on your own. The advantage here is that everyone can profit from this.

From an environmental standpoint, open-sourcing ideas is the best way to help everyone. Trying to blame big brands for all the issues out there just doesn't balance out when you realize that their contributions are still minimal in comparison to what is truly out there.

Here's a great example of a company really doing its part. A U.S. shoe brand called All birds created a unique product: a sustainable version of EVA foam. What that means is their foam is used making sugar cane, not nonrenewable fossil fuels. Not only that, they made the formula open-source so anyone can utilize this special foam when trying to create products.

See how open sourcing can be positive for everyone? Anyone who wants to create something using a foam now has an ethical option that doesn't do as much damage as other types. This is just one great example of how open sourcing can really help impact positively.

After a series of incidents at a Starbucks, the company closed the doors of its 8,000 stores for a full day to go through a whole new training concerning racial bias and how their employees should identify and handle it, that way there wouldn't be any more issues of that type. Once that was complete, they made their new training open-sourced so that any other companies could follow through as well, or utilize them when performing seminars of their own.

That was a great way for Starbucks to give back to their community and make things easier. There is no excuse to not have this type of training when the content for it is open-sourced and now readily available. See how this puts the pressure on other brands to follow through in positive ways?

Open-sourcing ideas and strategies is a great way for brands to give back to consumers, by proving they do care and they want to change with the times. What matters to consumers should matter to brands, and that's a trend consumers are easily swayed by.

Just remember that this idea itself isn't new or contemporary by any means. Open-sourcing content has been around forever, it's just now become more lucrative and expected for brands to use.

Take for example Volvo, who invented the three-point seatbelt in 1959. Hoping to help enhance the safety of the public, they made that patent open-sourced so anyone could access and utilize it, thus improving safety standards across the board for vehicles.

Coming up with innovative solutions and sharing them with the world is a great way to make a name for yourself as truly caring for the future and the productivity of others.

Not only can it help when it comes to bringing in an audience of consumers, it just makes you feel good too. The competitive advantages really outweigh any potential losses on this one.

Augmented Reality (Fantasy)

Escapism is nothing new. The art of storytelling is probably the most basic essence of humanity and goes back millions of years, to the art painted in prehistoric caves and even Egyptian murals and hieroglyphics. Before words, there were stories, and afterward, there will be stories still.

People want to believe in something more than them, they want to get lost in a world other than their own and feel immersed within it, and pretend they are someone else for a while. That's where books came from, and comics, and television, and movies. Now we have grown even more advanced as a society and have augmented reality.

Now that we have smartphones and infinite access to media, escapism continues to translate to longer and more interesting aspects. Adults can end up just scrolling on their phone for more than eight hours a day. It's not surprising there are more sophisticated methods to forget reality for a while.

Augmented reality is used by more than 80 million Americans every day. What is augmented reality, you ask? Well, in a simple answer, it is everything you already use. It's a reality that is superimposed into your hand in your phone or on your computer.

It's when there are real-world applications in a virtual space, such as using your phones GPs to get places, or when you play video games or watch television. Pokémon Go is a bit more of an advanced example of AR usage, but it utilizes your phones location system to track and place video game elements in the real world for you to play. You can even take pictures of Pokémon overlaid in real areas.

Another great example is that there is now a self-guided tour via an app for visitors at the Louvre. It involves integrating modern technology with real-world surroundings, and it is a fantastic development.

Something more simple just includes using your virtual world to improve upon the real world. Brothers John and Hank Green run many different businesses, and they created a non-profit called "The Foundation to Decrease World Suck". They marketed properly toward the younger age bracket, and they do 24 hour live streams in order to promoted donations to various charities. That's just one way they used their brands to influence real-world action and it is nothing short of incredible.

Your brand doesn't need to incorporate anything as drastic, these are just examples of how augmented reality is available in the day to day life and how it can affect the world. Many of the older generations often see this as a negative thing, but those in the market of business truly understand this is just another trend meant to improve quality of life.

Applying the appropriate types of escapism to your brand is a great way to connect to consumers, and attract new ones. Relating it to their real-life with as something as simple as a hashtag is a way to engage them that was never possible before.

Augmented reality is more than just the virtual experience, it's what the virtual experience can do for the real-world application, and the possibilities are endless. Find out what appeals to your niche, your audience, and you, and then see about incorporating it into your business model.

Chapter 12 Social Media Approach in Dropshipping

Social Media Marketing approach

A successful business does well marketing on public streets but the truth is since we are entering a new age of electronic future businesses must make haste for their change if they haven't gotten to it yet. This next change is to discover the new world of social media marketing. You are going to be reaching out online in many different ways. If there has been any previous advertisement experience had for the Business then one knows the power the word of mouth can bring.

Having social interactions with others build a great rapport with the individuals engaged. This kind of behavior is going to promote the global presence that the e-commerce shop has. Bringing in social media to an already online and trending topic is going to make with e-commerce a perfect pair. A business might have more than half of their following on a social media scale and thus in great odds will also make it easier to combine them into some good business marketing.

Bring the business to the front lines and where more than half the customers are; that's online. The web is going to be a strong motivator for content you are going to design your product line. Release a post about your new inventory and be descriptive when you tell the world that is going to pop and be a strong reminder to the visitors why they are going to visit your shop and ultimately why they will buy. Get started now and try making a social media account if you do not have one already.

There are tons of providers and many of them you will be able to market your business with. Create a login and finish editing the personal information on the account and everything that the business will be displaying to the public. Make the business account look nice and professional and it will attract business-like followers ready to see your catalog. Choose a provider that fits your needs or open two or many accounts to see which is going to work best for the business. The business owner may choose one social media outlet over another and this could give the business presence edge.

The only way to tell the right fit is to just jump right in and start designing. Social media has strong sources of the population that are willing to third-party market and this is why it's important to establish a bond with the community that surrounds. It can city-based or global to give back in many ways as long as you make the connection with your audience. Make their time worthwhile since they are spending so much online searching. Supply an online incentive that will encourage your audience to come back and share the content with other friends and family that are with them on these accounts. Find important partners that can also give you mentions and that will give you credible posts about the business you run and for many to see.

The question is can the e-commerce website survive from only social media marketing. This is not going to be a likely route because the only option the business has could lose it and have nothing left for support. If the company only dedicated their marketing budget to social media marketing, they are going to see the expensive cost burn through the budget quickly. Popularity is so important when it comes to running an efficiently visited shop but the company needs to take advantage of its capabilities to obtain followers from the social media sites that they could also be using, some of them even being free.

The more popularity you have the more profitable the business can be. The business can create very engaging motives towards their audience and they could attract more and more attention to the sites that are trickling into the shop daily. Keep gaining more followers and see what this popularity can do for the business.

Facebook Ads

Facebook ads are great and they are for any age range with a company structure. With Facebook as a company can market themselves from the bottom up and with little to no cost at all. Running Facebook ads can become costly if there is no following audience to broadcast to. If the company has no following on their web-sites then they are going to be paying money for company promotion and not for product promotion depending on how far we have gotten already.

These social ads are great because it engages thousands of people together for a common focus on the marketplace and this creates a strong playing field for posting products on any page. A company can pay for personalized ads that are going to air for the community to see sponsored posts on their pages and feeds so that they cleverly run into company products posted for great values. These advertisements cost the company upfront but they will also give great exposure to the presence of the shop.

The shop can post an ad about its new items or maybe marked down items that the company has extra inventory of. If the company can make an ad about the marked down items that are full in the inventory ware-house then products can be efficiently moved off of the warehouse shelves and into new revenue that is going to have the company break even with its assets. There has to be a balanced routine when it comes to paying for Facebook ads because not only can they get pricey but there will also be other ads that bring competition to the playing board.

It is in the best interest of the company to know exactly when to place an ad on the market. The company is going to need to be ready for any turnover and sales to skyrocket if necessary because if there is the right product niche the success is going to come pouring out. Customize ads with the company logo and titles that entice the customers to come on in and visit for the new sales. There is going to be opportunities to make a catalog or a flip advertisement and get creative with the cover flow when putting up an advertisement for the week.

Advertise on a good schedule so that none of the customers see the posts as spam and give the audience a chance to respond to the advertisement and give feedback about the current promotion. Utilize these ads when holidays come around and make an advertisement that speaks out above news in the Facebook place. This Facebook marketplace is going to create a level opportunity to see your posts and engage with the shop site that you like to involve in the posts. Ads can also be placed on the Facebook marketplace and this could include single items or bulk items.

This is a not usually the case because there are at times selling restrictions under certain sites but with Facebook ads this allows the company to list any variety of products. The company will be able to list products that can be sold as common goods or rare goods that are even handmade and at a limited source. Take advantage of the market diversity within Facebook because it will create a great opportunity to post and post again even when the product may not have sold the first week. If the product does not sell the first week through a Facebook ad markup the price and make the product bio look spiffier.

When the customers see that ad again they will have a new take on it and they will dedicate more time to considering visiting the shop site and picking out something that encouraged them to get there. With Facebook ads, it will be easier and easier for the average product supplier to have a global reach for the line in their shop. Global diversity is important so that every market genre can be tapped into and the company can take full advantage of selling their products to everyone around the world never missing a sale.

Google Adwords

With Google Adwords, there is going to be great diversity in search engines to bring plenty of crowds to the consumer website. With Google, Adwords google is going to place ads for the company on several landing servers and it is going to create ad space for all sites that are affected. Adwords is going to display ads for the company that relates to the company's mission or its makeup so that when someone is shopping or researching a site low and behold there will be an ad for the company and its product. This company ad is going to replace any space that may not have had an ad in the first place and this will create brand marketing for anyone who sees this ad.

Adwords control the ads that individuals see when they conduct searches like google searches for a specific product. This search is going to bring up many trending topics and depending on how much money the company decided to spend with AdWords the trending topic could the shop on a seasonal weekend. If the company is just starting Adwords is going to make a great opener for a company that has not built any brand advertisement. Lead a great advertising campaign by setting some money aside and spending it on advertisements every quarter to create a better-defined presence online.

This is going to maximize the reach the company makes on all of the audiences and this is going to ramp up production for any customers that have not seen or purchased from the shop yet. If product awareness can be brought to attention for the viewers all at once there could be a high spike of customers that come in to purchase all at once and this could send the company into a new stratosphere of sales. One of the main consistencies is the crowd flow and the amount of advertisement money spent which could be with Google Adwords.

Conclusion

Be prepared to take the skills that were learned in this book and transfer them into the next possible move in life which could be a Dropshipping business. You could be selling tee shirts or collectible seashells across the globe. Maybe your shop already has a company logo and now you want to do some brand marketing. Get aboard the Drop shipping train and enjoy the strategies you are going to learn through service providers like eBay.

Be aware that to run a great shopping website once you successfully take the plunge into creating a website for the company there is going to need to be security for every single piece of information that comes through the seller's website. Take care of these things with certificates that will encrypt your URL and links so that breaches will not try and attack the assets of your company and possibly even crash the whole site is complete and take everything.

Utilize marketing tools like Google Adwords and Facebook ads to gain full exposure to the community that you are engaging with. Remember that the community is going to be an online base so there needs to be consistency if the members begin to become forgetful. Entice them with special offers and make every customer feel great when they come to your shop so that they know they are getting more out of it than any other shop they will trust.

MAKE MONEY ONLINE WITH DROPSHIPPING

MAKE MONEY ONLINE WITH DROPSHIPPING: HOW TO GENERATE A PASSIVE INCOME OF $ 10,000 A MONTH USING THE DROPSHIPPING E-COMMERCE BUSINESS MODEL. LEARN THE SECRETS OF THE MOST SUCCESSFUL DROPSHIPPING BASED E-COMMERCE STORES.

Description

Have you always wanted your own e-commerce store but are worried about the cost and the risk? It is one of the biggest hurdles for people to overcome and most never get beyond the idea stage of having their own business and being their own boss. And understandably so; it can be expensive to start an online store and spend thousands purchasing stock, not to mention the risk of the products not selling.

This is why dropshipping is an excellent way to get into the entrepreneurial world and start earning an income through a business of your own. Dropshipping lets you sell products without actually having to purchase any products beforehand. In other words, you set up an online store, you list the products you want to sell, and when a customer buys something, you then place an order with the supplier who then ships it out to them. You then pocket the difference between what your customer paid and what it cost you to buy the item and get it shipped. You never need to buy stock and you never need to handle packaging and shipping – the supplier does all of that for you.

Dropshipping has provided people with an opportunity to have their own business that doesn't involve a big capital investment nor high risk. Want to know how it's done? Then read on. This book explains everything you need to know about how to set up a store, find suppliers, reach an audience and find new customers, and how to keep running your business once its active. It also suggests apps you can use to make your business more efficient and streamlined and marketing tools to help build your online presence and make your business successful.

The reason I wrote this book is to gather my knowledge on a subject I know a lot about based from personal experience and share with others in order to inspire them to take the plunge and set up their own business. With drop shipping, it's fairly straight forward and you can be earning a six-figure income in a matter of months, giving you independence and financial security.

This guide will focus on the following:

- Understanding dropshipping
- Why invest in dropshipping?
- What you need for a successful dropshipping business
- Setting up your dropshipping business
- The advantages of retail arbitrage
- How to pick the right products
- Find a supplier
- Contacting suppliers
- All about orders
- Affiliate marketing
- Scaling up your FBA business
- Avoiding common dropshipping mistakes... AND MORE!!!

Introduction

Earning a passive income online gives you the unique and incredible opportunity to maximize your income and step into the blissful world of financial freedom. When you are able to produce a six-figure online business that requires little of your involvement for maintenance, you eliminate your need to stay in the struggle and grind of a 9-to-5 corporate job. You open up your window of opportunity and give yourself the chance to live a life that is free, effortless, and bountiful.

Dropshipping companies are an incredible way to tap into the online retail industry without having to spend a great deal of money to get started. They are one of the best opportunities for anyone to take advantage of as very little is required in order for you to get started. To start, you simply have to set up your website or use a hosting website, plug in some products from qualified drop shipping wholesaler suppliers, and start marketing your business! Through effective management strategies and strong marketing techniques you will inevitably establish a business that will earn you a major income, up to six-figures and beyond!

There are many valuable benefits that you can enjoy if you start a drop shipping company of your own. Some of these benefits include: low overhead and zero need to carry inventory, low startup costs, and convenient automation systems. This business opportunity is truly one of the best ones available to anyone who is seeking to make a major income from the online world of e-commerce. Regardless of where your launch point is, you can definitely create a business that will earn you a massive amount of income.

This guide will guide you through absolutely everything you need to know in order to begin your own successful dropshipping business. You will learn about how you can begin your business, how you can manage your business, how to market your business, common mistakes to avoid, various tips and tricks to launch your business into success, and so much more. By the end of this book, you will have all of the skills and confidence that you need in order to cultivate your own business and earn a massive profit as a result. All you have to do is implement the simple-to-follow steps and watch your business grow!

If you are ready to release the caged lifestyle of a 9-to-5 job that requires excessive amounts of time and effort and start earning a passive income online, then you are ready to design your own drop- shipping business. Each chapter has been specially designed to ensure you have all of the tools you need to succeed with your dropshipping business. As you read, be sure to complete the suggested activities so that you can maximize the success you experience with your business. Finally, please enjoy.

Chapter 1 Understanding Dropshipping

Many people in the online space are talking about dropshipping companies. The idea sounds amazing: you don't carry any inventory and you use a host website (or your own) to earn a major profit. Before you get started, however, it is important that you know as much as possible about what dropshipping is and how it works.

What Is Dropshipping?

Dropshipping is a method of retail fulfillment that takes the requirement of carrying inventory off of the store owner. In traditional stores, even online, retailers are required to carry inventory so that when a sale is made they can ship the product to the purchasing customer. With dropshipping, however, the sale is fulfilled by a warehouse that carries stock for the store owner. Drop shipping warehouses are typically third party companies that are responsible for supplying stock to several different companies.

Because of the setup of a drop shipping store, the merchant is never required to see, touch, or carry inventory for the purpose of business. At most, the merchant may purchase samples to ensure the quality of the products they are selling on their retail store.

How Does It Work?

When a merchant stocks their online store with dropshipping-supplied products, the store is set up identical to any other retail store. You can go on a host website (such as Shopify) or go to the merchant's own web hosted store, which will show off all of the products that are for sale. From there, you decide what you are seeking to purchase and then you put it in your cart. Once you check out, the merchant is paid, and then the merchant automatically pays the drop-shipper for the product. The drop-shipper then ships the product to the paying customer, and the chain is complete. Aside from hosting the actual sales, the merchant is not involved in any of the rest of the process.

Will I Actually Make a Profit?

Due to a lower startup cost, lower overhead, and the ease of setting up a website online, it is actually extremely simple to make a profit from drop shipping companies. You simply create a website, host sales, and get paid every time someone purchases products from your website. You can host as many or as few products as you desire, and you can set the prices to whatever your desired price range is. As a result, you have a large amount of control over how much you will profit from each sale.

What Else Do I Need to Know?

Dropshipping is one of the easiest online businesses to run. You are not required to do a significant amount of work in order to maintain your shop, which means it is a highly passive income stream. Despite this fact, there is still work you will need to put into hosting your website or sales and ensuring that they succeed. Throughout this book, you will learn how you can operate your drop shipping business for the highest benefit. You can either be highly involved or outsource everything and have minimal involvement in the process. Ideally, especially if you are just starting out, you will want to be more involved so that you gain maximum profit. As you grow, then you may consider outsourcing even more of the work.

Dropshipping is a sophisticated opportunity to host an online retail store. It makes shopping online easy for both the merchant and the customer. It is highly cost effective and can be accomplished by virtually anyone who desires to create an online business and start earning money from it. You are not required to have any special talents when it comes to hosting a drop shipping retail store and earning profits from it, you simply need a willingness to learn and a basic understanding of the internet.

Chapter 2 Why Invest in Dropshipping?

Although dropshipping profit margins generally range between 15% and 45%, luxury items and consumer durables like electronics and jewelry may yield 100% profit margins. It all depends on selecting the correct niche and finding the correct supplier for it and making an entry into a market which is not saturated with it already.

Using a manufacturer to supply the goods directly rather than a supplier or vendor can cut out the role of a middleman and thereby ensure higher profit margins.

Once the enterprise gains momentum and establishes itself, it can almost become a money minting machine which does not require much input. The drop shipping business owned by Irwin Dominguez is an outstanding example of an e-commerce enterprise which earned one million US dollars in a very short span of 8 months. It gives an idea of the latent potential of this business.

Is Dropshipping For You?

Dropshipping is a fantastic option for new arrivals in the world of e-commerce. It requires a low-investment and involves less risk. These features can be enchanting and enthralling for the first-timers who are just stepping into the field of online business.

This type of enterprise demands a very small size of capital, so it is an ideal choice for those who already own a store and an inventory as well. They can try out certain goods in the markets and find out how they perform before getting a big stock of those goods.

The people who aspire to get impressive profits right away may not find this model very satisfactory. In case, your main goal is to earn a profit then it is better to associate with the manufacturers directly. But the catch is that the manufacturers do not always provide the facility for dropshipping.

The profit margins in this type of business are relatively lower than the other models of business, like wholesaling and manufacturing. In drop shipping a brand which is a fresh startup may not do well because the final control over customer satisfaction by means of brand experience and branding does not rest with the retailer.

Some facts and figures that show dropshipping is a feasible business model.

- *22% to 33% of retailers who work online have adopted the drop shipping business model.*

- *In 2011, 34% of the goods that were sold through Amazon were dropshipped. That means products worth more than $14 billion were dropshipped from a single online marketplace.*

- *Average profits of manufacturers who dropship their products are calculated to be 18.33% more than that of manufacturers who use the traditional retail business models.*

- *E-commerce sales on a global level were more than $2 trillion. It is anticipated that it will* *increase further and become nearly four and a half trillion dollars by 2021.*

Google Trends also shows that in the last few years there has been a massive rise in the number of people who are interested in the dropshipping business.

The Entrepreneurs for whom Drop shipping is Suitable

New Entrepreneur

Dropshipping is a chosen model for the people who are just taking the initial steps to sell things online. Basically, selling things online is not a cake walk. It takes time for an average marketer to learn and acquire a knack of driving traffic to his website and things like conversion optimization. This model gives them an inexpensive way to learn all this before making huge investments in the business.

Validating Entrepreneur

The dropshipping model is an amazing way to try out new products and startups. This type of business is perfect for entrepreneurs who need product validation prior to making any investments.

Walmart Entrepreneur

Dropshipping happens to be an ideal enterprise for people who wish to put up a wide assortment of items for sale. In a traditional form of business, it is not possible to sell many different items without spending a huge amount in acquiring an inventory. While this model can be used most suitable for this purpose without purchasing anything upfront.

Budget Entrepreneur

This kind of enterprise involves the least expenditure for selling things online as there is no necessity for purchasing an inventory. Therefore, it is a number one business model for entrepreneurs with a small budget or those who prefer to maintain the startup costs at a minimum level.

The Entrepreneurs for whom the Dropshipping Model is not Appropriate

Brand Oriented Entrepreneur

No doubt, establishing a long-lasting brand is a difficult task, but it is very rewarding. In the drop shipping business, it is even tougher to accomplish this task. The reason is that as a retailer you do not have much control over the factors which influence the customer experience.

For instance, there may be times when your customer purchases a product from which is already sold out by your supplier. You may feel uncomfortable and frustrated in such situations and find it difficult to coordinate the transactions between your supplier and the customer. This may prove to be a very unpleasant experience for the client.

Another way in which you do not hold the reins of your customer's experience is related to packaging. As the delivery part depends on the supplier, he may not put in much effort to please the customer with impressive packaging. Most of the time the items will be received by the customer in some ordinary brown box which is not a very attractive offer.

Moreover, as you do not ship the items yourself if a customer does not get the parcel you have to call the shipping company and settle matters. This may take a long time because you will have to deal with some busy representative of the company. Thus, you may not be able to satisfy the customer and get a good reputation.

An Entrepreneur Who Focuses on Margins

Most probably the most prominent issue associated with dropshipping is that there are very thin margins. Usually, the gross margins, that means the difference between the price at which you sell an item and the money you pay to the drop shipper, for traditional drop shipping goods are between 10% to 20%.

Advantages of Dropshipping

There are several aspects of this type of enterprise which are very advantageous. They are:

1. It can be set up very easily: You do not have to waste time and energy on assembling things and setting up the business. Just a few basic steps have to be taken to become a full-fledged trader. Put your best foot forward and choose a product, find a supplier, create a website for yourself, and sell your goods, that's it! Even a novice who is unfamiliar with the e-commerce enterprises can understand and follow these steps quite easily.

2. The amount of money required for setting up an online business is negligible: The traditional models of business involve a lot of investment to set up and perform the retail functions, for example, purchasing a space and inventory. This step is not necessary for dropshipping. So, the entire cost of setting up a physical business entity is eliminated. At most, you may have to invest money for running the website which includes the cost of hosting, apps, theme and other things.

3. No need to be concerned about huge overhead costs: It goes without saying that the businessman does not have to bear the financial

burden of paying the rent, phone bills, electricity bills pertaining to the office space or warehouse, or on buying stationery. You only need to think about managing the website and its fixed costs.

4. This type of enterprise involves less risk: You are not under any pressure to sell the products. You do not lose anything if your goods are not sold. If you cannot scale the store or earn profits, you can simply back out. So, the drop shipping model is a less risky form of business.

5. It does not depend on a location: You can carry on your business from anywhere. Therefore, you can be free from the hassles of maintaining an office, employees, and a warehouse. Since the business is independent of the location and is not tied to some concrete space, you can sit on a beach, or travel to your favorite resort and still make profits.

6. You can sell a varied assortment of products: It is possible to find a drop shipping supplier for nearly everything that you may wish to sell. There are so many options to choose from. You may rely on a single incredible product, sell different goods at the same time, or mix the popular products with the less popular ones. You are the master of your choice. All you have to do is select your niche. You will surely find a supplier for it.

7. You have more resources and time to augment your business: Traditional business models of business require more investment of resources and more work to earn more profits. While in drop shipping you just need to send a larger number of orders to the dropship supplier. The

supplier will do the rest for you. But all the profits will be credited to your account.

It takes less time to manage a drop shipping business, and it is almost automated. Consequently, you have more time on your hands to make plans and boost your business.

8. There will be less damaged goods and less loss: Goods are shipped directly by the suppliers to the buyers. So fewer shipment steps are involved. This greatly decreases the chances of damaging the goods while moving them from place to place.

9. It is convenient for the retailer and the supplier: The retailer does not have to bear the burden of packaging and shipping the products. The supplier does not have the responsibility of promoting and marketing his products. Both of them gain decent profits in the business. So, the drop shipping model is convenient for both of them.

10. Work with multiple suppliers: It is possible for the drop-shippers to work with a number of wholesalers at the same time.

11. Easy to scale or remodel: They can be scaled easily both vertically and horizontally. Drop shipping stores are totally digital. They do not need a place to keep the stocks. So, it is easy to scale them. Moreover, if one product or niche does not sell well, the retailer can conveniently switch over to some items which sell better.

12. No need for spending on an inventory: The retailer does not have to buy a product until he sells it and is paid for it by the customer.

In fact, the retailer has access to an unlimited inventory. If the supplier has an item, the retailer can easily put it up for selling on his website without spending any extra money.

Disadvantages of Dropshipping

But every coin has two sides. The downside of the drop shipping model of business is:

1. The profit margin is slightly lower compared to those of a wholesaler and manufacturer: According to your requirements, location, or niche, the vendors or suppliers may charge higher rates for drop shipping the goods. This impinges on the profit margin to some extent.

2. The liability for the entire transaction rests on the retailer: The customer purchases the item from the website of the retailer. The goods are sold in his name. So even if the supplier makes a mistake, the retailer is held responsible for it. Therefore, it is extremely important to select the right person as your supplier.

3. The retailer has less control over the packaging: Usually, a customer's satisfaction is linked with the personalized branding and packaging of the goods that are shipped. The small details like the notes and freebies that are given with the order make a lot of difference.

Unfortunately, the retailers do not get a chance to decide the way in which the goods will be presented at the time of delivery. This part of the transaction is mainly dependent on the supplier's choice.

Nevertheless, you can ask your supplier to brand things in a particular way. But you may have to pay some extra money for this service.

4. Some problems may arise because of shipping complications: It is a good idea to sell multiple items to increase sales and thereby boost your profits. But in case, you have a number of suppliers who supply different things this technique may prove to be counter-productive.

Different suppliers charge different rates for shipping according to the location, kind of goods, and some other factors. By chance, if a particular customer orders a number of things which have to be shipped by different suppliers, it will be a difficult task for the retailer. He will be required to calculate and pay the charges for shipping separately to each supplier. If he transfers the various shipping costs to the buyer, it will have a negative impact, and the profit margin may go down.

5. There is a lot of competition: The dropshipping model is very lucrative and popular. So, the number of sellers in every niche and segment is also large. Until a retailer caters to a very specific niche or segment the competition can be detrimental.

6. It can be a tricky affair to manage the inventory: It is almost impossible to keep an account of the supplier's stock. Lack of proper communication or wrong messages could lead to cancellations or delays. Although it is possible to tackle such problems with the help of software, it may increase the overhead costs and prove to be expensive.

Chapter 3 What You Need for a Successful Dropshipping Business

An Online Store

This may seem obvious, but you will need an online store to start your drop shipping business. Of course, you can always use a physical store as well, or maybe you already have one, but an online store is necessary so that people can see all the items you have to order.

I know, I know, for some people that seems like a heck of a lot of work to put into your business, but it's worth it, trust me. You see, this online business gives you the chance to expand beyond your local market.

An online store is not difficult to make, there are plenty of instruction manuals out there to begin with, or you can hire a designer to get you started and teach you how to key in your products. If you already have a physical store then it is an especially great idea to get started in dropshipping, as you won't need to also work on packaging and distributing the products. Seriously, there is no downside to this.

If you are not already the owner of a physical store with an online website to attach to it, then you can make your own online store. But starting a store from scratch can be a complicated business, though there are many sites you can work through that help such as Shopify and blank.

But there is also the possibility of buying an online store that already exists and then expanding from there. This option is really only viable if you happen to have the capital to invest into it, and since one of the appeals of drop shipping is a lower startup cost, then this might not be your number one idea.

When it comes to either designing your new online store or purchasing one, you need to take quite a few things into account.

- Professional look: this is important. You don't want your online store appearing all cluttered and confusing with pop-ups and ads everywhere. That can definitely dissuade people from shopping there. A more clean-cut appearance is desirable, and having your website look like a newbie designed it just won't cut it.
- Ads: Ads are a great way to add in revenue, but make sure it is tasteful and not taking up half the page.
- Mobile site: Most people shop online on their phones these days, so don't skimp when it comes to having a mobile option so people can seriously shop on the go. If the site isn't mobile-friendly then people are more likely to keep scrolling elsewhere.
- Choose Quality Retailers: We will discuss this further on in the chapter, but just know that you need to have reliable retailers. This is because even though you won't be the one shipping things out, the consumer sees you and your website as the responsible party overall, and it will affect them choosing to do business with you.
- Payment Options: It is helpful to have multiple payment options in an online store because then the customer has a quicker and easier experience when checking out. Using sites like Pay-pal or After-pay are a great way to appeal to wider audiences. Amazon also has one-click purchase options once

an account has been made with payment info, and that's another possible avenue you can take.

There are many different ways you can set up your online store, and the direction you choose is ultimately up to you. Just make sure you understand what you are really trying to sell with it, and have that brand match it.

With the right amount of dedication and knowledge, you can easily make your online store shine so that consumers find it easy to navigate. Having them want to use your store first is the best goal overall. Don't leave your customers disappointed and you will soon find that your revenue is coming in strong.

A Marketing Plan

This should definitely be a given, but some people don't take into account how necessary a marketing plan is to truly find success. Diving in sometimes feels like the most exciting part of beginning your new business adventure, but it isn't always sparkles and sunshine.

Not to take the wind out of your sales, but it's time to buckle down and get real.

On average, people want to go into business with whatever they are passionate about, be it books or pop culture or maybe even fishing supplies. But sadly that isn't always what will work best. What needs to be taken into account is what is in demand right now, and what you can sell. Focusing on a single passion or niche might not work in your favor because the quantity is chosen over quality these days.

Business and profit mean that you need to be realistic. It is possible to fulfill your passions while also making money, but it takes a good marketing plan to set that into effect.

Choosing what Market you want to focus on makes it easier to design your marketing plan, because once you know what products you know who you are trying to sell to.

Thanks to this beautiful era of the internet, there is so much information available at your fingertips, so utilize that well. There are all sorts of websites out there that talk about product trends, and even list out what is popular and selling well and why. Study up on what you might want to sell, and pay attention to what does sell, and that's the beginning of your marketing plan.

It's great that you may be into, say, cat-themed products, but selling only cat-themed products isn't going to be very original or net you much money. You want to expand your audience to expand your profit margin.

A few great places to check on trends include:

- Find out what the usual volume of the order is for certain products. For example, if a product isn't ordered in a large volume then it's possibly not a product you want available, as it doesn't sell as well as other products. Of course, that can be time-consuming to go through, which is where the next option comes in handy.

- Google Trends can really help you know what is truly taking off in the here and now, and get you started on finding products to pad your online store with. You don't want to pick things based on what you like, which is what a lot of people mistakenly do. Instead, you will focus on the market and what everyone else wants.

- Check out websites that are already popular and see what type of products they have and how they set up their websites. You can definitely follow direction that way without copying word for word. Just get an idea of what appeals to your customer base. You can't ever go wrong with research.

Ultimately, research is what will help you form the best marketing plan directed toward your goals. You can't just jump the gun and think you'll be the next star of the dropshipping world. Take time to properly research the products and the message you are trying to give with your store.

Just remember not to focus too much on the trends themselves, just make sure they are available within your business. This is because trends change, and you won't have the time or revenue to revamp your store when trends change. Just make sure that the niche you focus on is one that has constant trends, and not something is unique jut for now.

Checking out your rivals is another great way to compare how you are doing your work. Your competitors are an important part of your business model because they are who you are actively working to be better than. If you know how your competitors are working and what tools they may be using then you are on the way to knowing how to compete with them.

If you follow these rules then you will be sure that consumers know exactly what they are getting with your business. This will also help make sure that you are not targeting a niche that will lead to failure.

Take a deep breath and start focusing on the plans for your future, because the right plans will always lead you on the path to greatness.

Reliable Suppliers

The next step? You guessed it! Finding reliable suppliers is quite an important part of setting up your drop shipping business. This one really speaks for itself because you don't want to have to worry about whether or not your customers will receive exactly what they believe they are purchasing.

As the online store that they are buying from, they will see your business responsible for any mishaps, even if they understand that they are buying from other retailers. This is because you are the go-between they are depending on, so the retailers you work with should be dependable and trustworthy from the get-go.

When you decide that you are ready to begin choosing suppliers, there is quite a lot that you need to think about. Consider first a suppliers popularity and dependability. There are various websites you can use to see reviews, ratings, and even how long they have been around.

You want to work with someone who is already established and who has a strong history of being reliable so that you don't have to worry about accidentally betraying your customers.

Proper research will always be important on your part and can make or break your business. If you choose suppliers willy-nilly then you are asking for mistakes to be made and money to be lost. Be proactive by doing this the proper way, even if it takes a little more effort.

Once you have a list of potential suppliers that look good, you can dig into the nitty-gritty of it all. That's right, you start asking suppliers the real questions and see what you can afford and what it would be like to work with them.

This means asking them things like shipping times, order minimums, and other business-related dealings, usually involving the money and transactions.

Once you've narrowed it down then it is time to do some practice orders with these suppliers, to see if they practice how they preach. If the order is wrong or doesn't match their claims, then you know they are not the business for you. That should make it easier for you to pick the one or two businesses you will want to start working with first.

It's definitely possible to have multiple retailers to work with but that should be saved for once you have a better handle on your business. Biting off more than you can chew isn't recommended if you are looking for success.

There are many different methods for getting where you want to be with your drop shipping business, you just need to stick with us and read through all the knowledge we have to share. There is no one-step route to this, you need to be ready to put the time and effort into it.

Ecommerce is a fun and competitive market to work in, and you should be excited that you are going about it the right way. Be ready to break into the market and start finding success around each corner, just like you have always dreamed of.

Understanding the Common Pitfalls of a Dropshipping Business

While we would love for the drop shipping business to be a rollercoaster that only goes up, that just isn't the case, and we'd be liars if we avoided discussing the downs of the business. There are quite a few common pitfalls of a drop shipping business that you should be aware of and prepared for.

It's quite common to get too excited and forget the reality of what you are doing, which is: running a business. You need to remember that there will be lots of drops as you go, and it will be a true rollercoaster ride. Here are some of the things to expect from your dropshipping business that are less than stellar:

- Huge competition. That's right, since the internet is infinite that leaves almost an infinite amount of competition, which means it is even more difficult for you to find ways to truly stand out from your competitors. It isn't too difficult to start a drop shipping business and it requires less money than many other types, which makes it appealing to many people who aren't really willing to do their research first. The competition can be killer if you don't prepare for them in whatever type of products you are selling and the prices that you need to match to appeal to the consumer. You are also a small business competing with a large business, who's able to take bigger cuts on profit than you are. That's why it's so important that you choose your market carefully.
- Not as simple as you first believe. Seriously, it seems like the dream idea because you don't have to do the physical work yourself, but there is still plenty that needs to get done. When you don't have a physical inventory it can really complicate things. If a customer orders multiple items from different suppliers, it is then up to you to figure out what that means for them when it comes to calculating shipping, or whether you offer discounts when it comes to that. Some businesses do free shipping

if you order a certain amount from the same supplier, so that is a possibility to take into account.

- You haven't experienced the products yourself. Not being able to touch or examine what you are selling can have its downside when it comes to customers who have questions about the product, or even when you are writing up your product descriptions and sales pitches. You need to make sure you know that you can be engaging about a product and also be well informed.

- You aren't in control of the shipping. This is one of the most popular parts of running a drop-shipping business, but this can also be your downfall. This is because your business is the face selling the product, so if something goes wrong or shipping messes up, you can't just throw the blame on the supplier and wipe your hands clean of it. You need to be able to communicate effectively with both the customer and the supplier and know the answers to questions before they are asked. That can take a lot of time and dedication.

- Legal issues. Yes, legal issues definitely can arise when it comes to dropshipping. This is why you always need to have a contract when you strike up a partnership with a supplier. If they are involved in illegal activities or have misrepresented themselves or their products then you are considered complicit as well.

- How much you order is up to you. This isn't always the case, because shops will require a minimum order when it comes to doing business with them, so they can weed out those who could end up wasting their time. You also can realistically only order as much as they happen to have in stock at the time, and they may not give you as much as you want either. You are competing with other businesses out there who are also buying supplies, and they might rather put more of their stock into businesses they know have a good return.

There are many more issues that can arise when it comes to running a dropshipping business, but these are just some of the more common ones we wanted to run over first.

Chapter 4 Three ways to run a functional dropshipping store

There are two main popular ways to run a dropshipping store and one unpopular approach – let's talk about the three of them briefly. The first method or approach is to create a storefront on any of the popular e-commerce platforms. Once you have created the store, you need to research and find hot selling products and then list them on the store. When people order the product, you send their information across to a supplier to fulfill the order for you.

One advantage of having your dropshipping store on already established marketplaces is that you get to leverage the brand image of the e-commerce platform to sell more. Online shoppers already have a good perception of the major online e-commerce marketplaces. So, once you have a store on such marketplaces, the brand image rubs off on you. This means that a buyer would be more than likely to purchase from you.

For instance, Amazon is a well-recognized e-commerce marketplace – the platform is also well known for its customer satisfaction policy. Now, if you create a drop shipping storefront on Amazon, an online shopper will trust your store just for the mere fact that it is on Amazon or that it has Amazon's branding on it.

The role that branding or brand image plays in the success of a business can never be underestimated. So, if your store has a positive brand image as a result of its association with Amazon (associative branding), then you are sure to gain the trust of your potential buyers and record more sales.

Another advantage of having your drop shipping storefront on established e-commerce marketplaces is that you get to enjoy the enormous traffic that gets to such platforms daily. There is no doubt that platforms like Amazon welcome a barrage of human traffic every day. And all those visitors are on the platform for one thing – which is to buy something. If you position your store before such a vast audience, then you are sure to record sales.

With the type of traffic that gets to the platforms, you may not need to spend huge amounts of money on advertising your products or store. Yes, you may still need to pay some money to the different platforms for improved visibility, but that would be significantly lower than the amount you would have spent on PPC (Pay per Click) advertising, for instance, if you were trying to pull your own traffic to the store.

The only disadvantage or rather drawback that comes with selling on popular e-commerce marketplace is that the competition can be stifling. Since it is pretty easy to create a storefront on those platforms, the competition is quite high as there are many vendors jostling for the traffic that comes to the sites.

However, it is essential to note that competition is a normal part of running a business. There is no type of business that does not face competition, but your ability to position yours uniquely is what will differentiate your store from the millions of others that are available.

Another way through which you could run a drop shipping store is to create your own independent online store and then connect it to an order fulfillment platform like Shopify. To go with this approach, you will have to buy a domain name, hosting package, and then design your store from scratch.

After designing the store, you will then populate it with products. Some plug-ins allow you to automatically import products from various order fulfillment sites into your own online store. Using such plug-ins or software applications will make the job of populating your store with as many products as possible easy for you.

Note: as a drop-shipper, it is essential for you to add as many products as possible to your store. The more products you add, the more your sales. Remember, we said earlier that drop shipping thrives on volume sales. Since you are not even the person fulfilling the orders, you don't have to bother about the stress of fulfilling many orders at once.

The major advantage of creating your own independent dropshipping store is that you are entirely in charge of your business. If you create a store on a popular marketplace like Amazon or eBay, you could wake up one morning to find that your store has been deleted or restricted. If another company can delete or restrict your business, then it is safe to say that you don't have a business. Running your own independent store puts you in control. You decide the types of products you want to list on your store and those you don't want.

A significant disadvantage of running an independent store is that you would have to do your own branding yourself. Getting prospects to trust your store and leave their money with you can be a hard task. You will work extra hard before you could gain the trust of your audience. This is unlike what happens when you are selling on a popular marketplace – the brand image of the marketplace serves as an umbrella that covers you.

Another disadvantage of running your own independent drop shipping store is that you will have to spend a lot of money on marketing. You will be responsible for driving traffic to your store, and this can often be expensive. Running PPC campaigns all the time can take a huge toll on your income and reduce your profit significantly. And unless your store has become very popular, you will always need to run ads for people to keep coming to your store.

The third, albeit unconventional method to run a drop shipping store, is the social media approach. This involves showcasing high in demand products on social media – when your followers or other social media users like any of the products you have displayed, they would order them. You will then need to source for a supplier who will deliver the product to the online shopper.

This type of dropshipping could best be described as manual drop shipping although some people would choose to call it retail arbitrage. Many drop-shippers usually start their journey on social media and then proceed to build their own platforms or create stores on e-commerce marketplaces.

One major advantage of this dropshipping approach is that it is the least expensive option. You don't pay any money to create a post on social media. It is also easy – you are not required to set up anything. Any regular social media user can create posts and ask people interested in a product to get in touch.

A major disadvantage is that you will have to gain the trust of your followers first before they are willing to do business with you – and this can take time. Also, you will need to grow a large social media following – again; this can take time. If you want to work with social media influencers (people with large social media following), you will have to spend a lot of money.

Another disadvantage is that your business will be at the mercy of the social media platform in question. The social media platform that you are using could decide to restrict the number of your followers who get to see your ad posts. If that happens, you will have to run PPC campaigns, which can be quite expensive.

Often, people who are new to dropshipping do ask, "Which is of the three approaches is best for a newbie?" There is no straightforward answer to that question – some drop-shippers start with social media while others start with e-commerce marketplaces. It depends on you and the level of technical knowledge you have. You could even start with your own independent store if you are sure of what you are doing.

Since we have looked at the different ways of running a drop shipping store, let's proceed to talk about how to actually create and run one. But before then, let's summarize some of the reasons why drop shipping is excellent for every e-commerce entrepreneur.

Why bother about dropshipping?

Here are a few reasons why you should consider starting your own dropshipping business today:

1. It is easy to start

As mentioned earlier, starting a new business used to be hard – however, business models like drop shipping have made owning a business a simple process. As a drop-shipper, you don't need to worry about getting office space; you don't have to worry about hiring and paying staff; at least when you are just starting. You may need to hire virtual assistants to assist in running the business later, but that's when you have grown to a reasonable extent.

Furthermore, you don't have to bother about securing huge startup capital – essentially, you are not using your money to run the business. You are only but a middle man, you take money from an online shopper, pay some of the money to a supplier of a product, and you keep the remaining as your profit. So, you don't need huge funds – if you already have a computer or even a mobile phone and an internet connection, then you could start and grow a drop shipping store.

Since you don't fulfill your own orders yourself, you don't have to worry about product research and development. The product's supplier has already done an excellent job of researching and developing the right product so that the burden is no longer on you. If a product stops selling well, you will only need to research and find other hot-selling products and list them on your store. As you may already know, product research and development is one of the most challenging aspects of running a business. But as a drop-shipper, that aspect is already taken care of. So, you are hugely in luck.

Once you have found a good product that you want to sell, you only need a platform to display them or make them visible to buyers. You could leverage existing and already trusted e-commerce marketplaces to display your products, or you could create your own independent online store. Social media is also a great place for displaying the products you are selling.

2. Easy access to millions of products

As a drop-shipper, you could list thousands of products on your store and make more money. The more products you list, the more your chances of recording sales, which translates to more money for you. Listing as much as a thousand products on your store is practicable since you are not the one developing the products or fulfilling the orders.

You are not restricted to one type of product – you could source for products from different suppliers and list them on your store. Whenever a product is ordered, you simply send the order details to the affected supplier to fulfill the order. To list different products, you just need to create different sections on your store, especially if it is an independent store. For instance, you could list headphones, totem bags, phone cases, belts, shoes, etc. on the same drop shipping store.

3. You can set the price of products

A supplier will often give you products at wholesale or reduced prices – you could then add your own profit to the cost and sell to the buyer. If you desire to make more money, you could raise your prices slightly while ensuring it is still reasonable.

4. Easily scalable

As a drop-shipper, you can easily scale up your business by hiring virtual assistants to assist in the running of the business. You could also create more stores on other marketplaces where you don't have one already. You could research and list more products to increase your profitability.

Downsides

Dropshipping has its own downsides – so, it is essential that we also mention some of them. Without romanticizing everything, here are some of the disadvantages of dropshipping:

1. High competition

If you have a store on any of the popular e-commerce marketplaces, which is what most drop-shippers do, then you will have to deal with stiff competition. Drop shipping has a very low barrier of entry – it is a business which anybody can join – and as expected, the competition is very high. However, you could always overcome competition by developing unique strategies. And you have to understand that there is competition in every business. Even those businesses that have a very high barrier of entry still face competition.

So, you have to see competition as a regular thing in business and work out strategies on how to stand out from the crowd. The best way to beat the competition in drop shipping is to find and sell unique products that many people are not already selling. Most drop-shippers have a herd mentality – once they hear that one item is selling like hotcakes, they will all rush in to sell the same product. Do not be like most drop-shippers; you should be different if you ever want to stand way above the competition.

2. Supplier error

Sometimes, you order a different thing, and the supplier sends an entirely different item to your buyer. This happens more often – and in such situations, the buyer might escalate the situation and hurt your business. Supplier error can make you lose money as you will need to use your money to pay for the actual product that the buyer wanted.

3. Shipping times are usually longer

Most suppliers are based in distant countries like China – as a result, ordered products will often take a longer time to get to the buyer. While many buyers do not care about long shipping times, some others will not take it. Some potential buyers will not purchase from your store if they discover that the shipping time will be longer than necessary – making you lose out on money you would have made.

The above are just some of the downsides of running a dropshipping business. Despite these assume downsides, drop shipping is still a great business model for anyone who wants to become financially independent while keying into new global trends. If you are now convinced that dropshipping is for you, then read on as the next sections of this guide will take you by the hand and show you how to create and grow your own e-commerce empire.

Chapter 5 How Much Money Will I Need to Start My Business?

This chapter will give you the good, the bad, and the ugly about dropshipping. While dropshipping is an excellent way to make money, there are some difficulties you may face. This chapter will help paint the overall picture to help you understand the drop shipping method more before you dive in. This chapter is especially important to read so you can figure out how to set yourself apart from your competition. This starts with your mindset which will be the subject of the next section.

The Successful Dropshipping Mindset

Sure, having your own business sounds good, but those who want to be successful as an online business owner must have a certain mindset. If you don't have this mindset, then you won't be able to make it. The mindset of a successful online business owner consists of four pillars.

1. The first pillar is that you must be committed to hard work. Some may even call you a workaholic and rightfully so. Business owners will put as much time as they need into their business. Successful business owners put in a lot of work. Sometimes they put in a lot of work before they even see results. This is not normal. Some people are afraid of hard work. They are always looking for the shortcuts in life to do the least amount of work possible. Business owners do the exact opposite. They understand that hard work is necessary to achieve their dreams. They

approach their journey to business ownership with the expectation that they are going to work hard. The hard work does not deter them, but rather the ability to not reach their dreams is more important than hard work. It's this obsessive commitment to hard work that drives business owners, and it is at the core of being one.

2. The next pillar of the business owner's mindset is the willingness to invest money in their business. Business owners know that to make a business run you have to invest money. Oftentimes, with limited resources, they find themselves investing their own money. They know how to save their money to help them make it through the lean times. They have the discipline to put their money back into their business instead of spending it. They use the money that they make to work for them. They are quick to learn and use the info to make more money.

On the other hand, investing money in their business can also be a business owner's downfall. If a business owner is investing too much money into a sinking ship, they are not being smart. However, successful business owners know when it's smart to stop investing their money, but they are not afraid to spend it. Even if they spend too much money into their business, they are able to quickly make adjustments in the best interest of their business.

3. The next important pillar of being a business owner is knowing how to focus their time wisely. Working hard is important, but if you work hard on things that do not matter to your business,

then your work is pointless. Successful business owners know how to focus on the most important activities that help their businesses grow. They focus on the task that brings in money and outsource the rest. (More information about outsourcing will be given later in the book.) Once they figure out what activities make the most money for their business, they spend time on those tasks.

Successful business owners are master time management practitioners. It's easy to get sucked into the vortex of trying to do everything for your business. Successful business owners do the opposite. They focus on the most important things so they can have a well-rounded lifestyle. This commitment to focus and to manage their time allows them to stay on the business path longer than those business owners who try to do everything and find themselves being burned out.

4. The last important thing that successful business owners know how to do is be objective. Most people have a bias to their abilities and their efforts. This blind bias makes them take bad decision after bad decision, especially when it comes to their business babies. Business owners are objective about their expectations and goals when it comes to their business. They are able to see if what they're doing is working and don't get emotional about it. They can handle feedback constructively, but they are their most constructive critic. They take the feelings out of their business and look at the data to see if it supports what they are trying to do. If what they see supports their expectations and goals then

they continue to do those actions. However, if their expectations and those are not being met, business owners do not feel bad about taking a new path to reach those goals or modifying their expectations and reality. Unfortunately, many people have certain expectations about their business, but once they start working, they realize that those expectations don't correlate in the real world. People love to think about business but are shocked what happens when they actually do business.

Business owners are not so committed to their ideas that they are not able to change. They understand that the business is constantly changing, and they don't take the changes that their business may show them personally. This ability to be objective helps them find the proper resources that will help their business to succeed. If they feel they are too close to the business, they don't mind asking mentors or hiring business coaches to be objective with them. Successful business owners know that being objective is the only way that their business can survive, and they seek out best information to help them measure their business against so they can survive long-term.

In conclusion, being a business owner is a dream that many have, but not many are willing to work for it. Having a successful business is not just selling your company for millions of bucks. Having a successful business means a commitment to excellence and lots of hard work reeling to meet your business's goals and expectations. In order to be a true business owner, you must have a foundation on a mindset consisting of four pillars. The first is a love for hard work; the second is a commitment to investing money in your business; the third is knowing how to focus on the money-making task of your business, and the fourth pillar is knowing how to be objective.

Business ownership is very rewarding, but there is hard work that goes into it. If you are willing to make the commitment, then you're going to have a lot of fun. If you're not sold on the hard work that it takes to be successful, then stop reading now. However, if you're up to the challenge, keep reading. Because drop shipping has become so popular, you have to brand your business well, which will be the subject of this next section, and one of the best places to begin.

Branding

Branding is a big decision. Every drop-shipper has to decide what they want their brand to be. Your brand has to be exciting, unique, and fit into your ideals. Your brand is important because it separates you from other companies. Some people have very strict methodologies about what type of brand name is most successful for a dropshipping company. Some people have a strict list of do's and don'ts. However, I believe the proper branding for your company is whatever you truly feel you want to do. It is not as hard as you think. The branding should speak to the product that you are selling. Many people have ideas for brands, but they are not sure about how to bring the idea to life. If you have purchased this book, then I'm sure you have already thought of an idea for a brand. This chapter will help you refine the branding idea that you already have or help you create a brand if you do not have one already. Initially, you should start off with strong branding because the brand will be associated with your business for a very long time. The branding consists of the physical assets such as the colors and physical imaging of your branding, like your logo. Your brand is also abstract as it is the story behind your company.

Two important components help determine what your branding will be. The first component is the brand concept or the idea for your business. The next component important to your brand is going to be your target market.

The idea behind your business is the brand concept. Simply put, the brand concept is about what your brand represents. To help form your brand concept, you should ask yourself a few important questions.

- When people see your brand, what ideas do you want them to associate with your brand? - Do you want them to think of youthfulness or maturity? Do you want them to think of free-spirited people or business-minded people? What other ideas do you want them to think about when they hear your brand's name or see your brand's imaging. There is no right or wrong answer to this. It is simply what you want your brand to be.
- What is your mission statement? - You may think a mission statement is a broad, detailed story, but it is simply what you want your company to do or be. What kind of goals do you want to reach with your company? Do you want to be the top grossing baby line company in the world or would you like to be the most successful luggage company in the world? Do you want to help stop poverty with a portion of your sales? Whatever your goal is for your company that is what your mission statement should be.
- What is your brand story? - Your brand story is different from your mission statement; although they may share some overlap. The brand story

talks about the origins of your company, whereas the mission talks about the goals of your company. You can incorporate your origin story or the initial idea that inspired you to start your company. People connect to a brand story because they are able to see themselves in the brand. Make sure that the brand story is written in a way that's relatable and truthful. It is a foundational aspect of your business.

- What colors do you want to represent your brand question? - Choosing the colors of your brand is very important. If your brand has a calm vibe, then you most likely will want a calm color to represent your brand. A fiery color like orange and red may not be ideal, but a cool color like blue or light green may be more ideal. However, there is no hard-and-fast rule for the colors that you choose. Your brand makes the color. Do not stress if your colors are like another business because there are only so many colors in the world, so a few businesses are bound to use the same kind. However, make sure that your colors represent your brand in a way that it is not used by another brand. That's where your brand story in your mission statement comes into play.
- What logo would you like to represent your brand? - Some people like to just use logos or initials to represent their brand. The type of font used in the logo is also part of the brand. There are lots of different companies that can help you develop your brand. A popular website to use is fiverr.com. The designers there will ask you questions, and you can brainstorm with them to

find your brand for cheap. Other people like to use free logos and add their own fonts with a website like Canva, which is another low-cost option.

Once you have your initial branding down, you will then want to think about your target market. They may influence your branding efforts as well. A great activity to do when trying to figure out who your target market is to create three brand identities of the people who will buy your product. This helps you to learn more about your customers, and find a brand that will appeal to them. It is important to know multiple types of customers you are targeting because different target markets will be attracted to your business for different reasons. Knowing your target audience may help you prevent a no-no. For example, if you have a vegan company, you may not want to have a bloody cow as your logo. Thinking about your customer can help you come up with cool ideas and ways that you can connect to them. When trying to figure out who your target market is going to be, you should do your research. You may realize that your idea may not work after you do research. However, these three brand identities will help you research further and find out more about your customer. It is important to note that when you begin, you will learn more about your customers. As the information comes in about who is buying your product, do not be afraid to adjust some of your branding efforts at the point.

When you think about the brand identities here are a few questions that you can ask.

- Where is your customer from? What country or continent are they from? What city in that country are they from?

- How old is your target demographic? Try to narrow this down as much as possible. Have one major segment and then another major segment for two major target demographics.
- Will your product solve a certain problem for them? Is your target demographic unable to find styles that work for them that your style will address?
- Does your product represent a certain ideal for them? Is your product brand the most expensive form of product that they can ever afford? Is it an urban style?
- Where does your customer stay most of the time when they are on the internet? Are they browsing social media or are they on news websites?
- How do you get your promotion in front of them? Are you going to use advertisements on a search engine or social media websites?
- What are their hobbies? What do they love to do already? What hobbies are they spending money on to do?
- What do they like to read? What genres do they like to read? Do they prefer audiobooks, printed books, magazines, or blogs?
- What do they like to eat? Are they vegan or do they love meat? Do they care about where the animals they eat come from?
- Are they healthy? Do they suffer from chronic illnesses?
- Are they married? Are they divorced? Are they in long-term relationships? Are they in homosexual or heterosexual relationships?

- Do they have children? How many? Are these children that they birthed? Are these children that they adopted? Do they have trouble conceiving?
- Are they homeowners? Or do they rent? What type of homes are they living in? Brownstones? Ranch homes?
- What type of interior décor is their style? Modern? Farmhouse? Contemporary? Chic?
- Do they travel? Do they travel domestically or internationally?
- Are they educated? If so, how much education do they have? What's the highest education they have?
- What do they do for a living? Are they blue-collar or white-collar workers?
- Do they have pets? Do they have dogs or cats? Or fish?
- What type of cars do they drive? Do they love luxury, hybrids, practical?
- What movies do they watch? What're their favorite genres?
- What TV shows do they watch? Are they watching cable or a paid service like Netflix or Hulu?

Forming a detailed profile and multiple profiles will help you to make connections with your target market in ways that you would not have done had you not been as detailed. Be as detailed as possible and look for connections. It will help you market to them as well. This step should not be taken lightly. Take the time to sit and think through this. You can give yourself a few hours in a room with a pen and paper or with your computer to take notes. Do not have any distractions.

Do not turn the TV on, and you can even turn your phone off. Having a very focused, niche target demographic can be the difference between success and failure. You can mark it to more than one target demographic. However, you have to start with at least one target demographic first. Build on one target demographic, have success with that target demographic, and then move to the next target demographic. Next thing you know you will be selling to lots of people. Just remember that you have to crawl before you walk.

Ultimately, the brand for your company is something you should not stress about because companies rebrand all the time. Starting the company is more important than letting your brand stop you from getting started. If all else fails, just focus on what products you would buy or products you are interested in and build your business from there. You can then build your brand identities from there. These three brand identities are a great place to start, and it will help you research further and find out more about your customer. If you have the money for it, you can also hire a brand consultant to do the heavy lifting for you. If you have local business accelerators in your city or an SBA office or any nonprofit that helps economic development in the city, they may have workshops for developing your brand. So be sure to take advantage of these free opportunities to get feedback about your business. The next section will focus on answering all the tough questions many people have before they begin dropshipping.

The Downright Ugly

Drop shipping can be competitive, and there a few ugly things you must know before you begin.

- Profits margins can be low. You may think that the best products to sell are the ones that are expensive, but you may be surprised that some of the best products to sell are lower-priced items. This is not a hard and fast rule, but something you should keep in mind. Try to find a drop-shipper that will let you get your product at the lowest price possible.
- Returns are inevitable. Most drop shipping businesses will have to deal with returns, so you have to decide how you are going to handle them. You have to decide if you are going to offer no refunds, or accept returns and handle shipping, or any other policy you would like to create.
- You are not in control of shipping. Because you are not the supplier, you are not in control of shipping as if you were shipping the products yourself. This is something you should be aware and create protections through the shipping policies and return policies of your business. Under promise and over-deliver!
- Shipping can eat your profits, especially if you're doing worldwide shipping. You will want to negotiate and research to find the best deal with shipping. Sometimes using the USPS is the most efficient option, and they have pretty labels, so don't overlook them.

- Failure can be high. If you don't choose the right product, or pick the right website build or the right marketing option or any of the million reasons that must be right for your business to succeed, you will fail. The best way to overcome failure is to do lots of research before you begin, monitor how much you are spending, and don't be afraid to make adjustments quickly. What you think may not always work, so don't be afraid to pivot if you see that something is not working.

Another Ugly Truth

Initially, you probably won't make much money. The first couple of months might not be profitable. However, if you can survive these first few months and begin to turn a profit, then you will be okay. You should keep detailed notes of your business sales and what you are making. For example, you can use an Excel spreadsheet to track your business expenses. Break down what everything will cost from shipping to what it costs to have your products manufactured to the packaging to the money you spent on advertisements. Keep it in a list. Then keep a daily count of how many sales you are making and what the orders are. That way you can see what products are most popular and reinvest in those products. You can also see if certain products are not making you any money.

Try to be as lean or spend as less as possible, then you can upgrade your business as you go. Try to make it out the first month so you can really start seeing a profit from what your orders are. Again, always reinvest your money back into the business and do things that work. So many people lose their business because they take too much money out.

If you see that you are not making as much money as you want initially, do not give up. Keep going. However, if you are burning through thousands of dollars every month, you may need to come up with a different strategy. And of course, everyone needs to have a point where they say I need to pivot before totally turning in the towel. Determine what the 'throwing in the towel' moment is for you. The most important thing is if something isn't working, learn from it and if you keep doing that you will find the winning strategy.

Answers to The Tough Questions

If I don't have any money, how can I begin a drop shipping business?

The great thing about drop shipping is that you don't have to have any money to get started. You can use a site like Zazzle or Tee-spring or another print-on-demand site and ask your friends and family to purchase a product from you there. Once you have enough money, you can then get fancier tools for your business. If your friends and family members have money, you can ask them for a loan or run a Kick-Starter or Go-Fund-Me for your beginning expenses. Because drop shipping does not cost a lot to get started, you can find someone to help you out.

What common mistakes should I look out for?

Drop shipping can fail because people do not take the time to do the proper research before they get starting. Here are a few things you should do to help your business succeed.

- Take the extra time to look into the competition: Drop shipping has become competitive so make sure you are differentiating yourself from your competition. Looking at what your competitors are doing is a great way to help you figure out how you will be different. Shopify has an entire marketplace you can look at to see what people are selling so you can compare notes.

- Do a test order from a supplier: Doing a test order will help you figure out how your supplier handles their orders. Some people avoid this step and have to pay the cost in the long-run. In the same vein, have a backup supplier that you should order from so you can always have a quality drop-shipper around. Ali-express and Ali-Baba aren't the only places you can find a drop-shipper. Don't skimp on the research state of finding a great drop-shipper or you will pay for it in the long run.

Should I focus on my passion or what will make me money?

This is a great question and one that is always asked no matter what business model someone wants to begin. If you can have a passion that is lucrative, that is ideal. However, this question depends on your long-term goals. If you want to make money, you should focus on a product you know that will sell, and if you want to focus on your passion, find a product that will sell and you enjoy. These techniques will be explored more in

How can I make sure that the quality of my drop shipping product is good?

You need to do a test order from your suppliers. Also, read the comments and look at the pictures that other people post. Having more than one quality drop-shipper is imperative. Again, please do not skip on this step.

What should I be thinking about long-term for my drop shipping business?

One of the best pieces of advice is to think with the end if mind. Do you should-sell your drop shipping business after a while? Do you should-give it to your children? Is this going to be a side business for you? Decide what your end goal is before you start building your drop shipping business so you can reach the goals and always have a big picture of what you need in mind. This will help you stay focused on your goals!

Great job on making it through this chapter! A lot of the principles covered in this chapter will help your drop shipping business start on the right foundation. Now that we have a strong foundation, we will move into the next concept of starting your drop shipping business which is to know about supplying and fulfilling.

Chapter 6 Setting Up Your Dropshipping Business

By now, I am sure that you have a clear understanding of drop shipping and how drop shipping orders are fulfilled. You have also selected a suitable niche, decided which products to carry in your store and identified the suppliers you are going to work with. Now, its time to move on to actually setting up your drop shipping business. However, before I take you through the process of building your business, there are a few things you need to know.

One of the things I have observed with first-time online entrepreneurs is that most of them make the mistake of assuming that building an online business is an easy process. When it comes to building a successful business, you have to adopt a long-term view and have a high level of commitment—regardless of whether it's a brick-and-mortar store or an online business. Because of the thousands of fascinating online business success stories on the internet, most people start an online business with very unrealistic expectations. If you aim to throw up a website, sit back, and expect to get a six-figure income in two months, you are going to be very disappointed. However, if you start with realistic expectations and a clear understanding of the amount of investment it will take to get you there, you will be less likely to quit when things get tough.

During the early stages of building your drop shipping business, you will have to make a major investment, either in time or money.

Investing Your Time

If it is your first time building a drop shipping business, I advise you to invest more time than money. Investing time in this crucial stage of your business will help you learn all the intricacies of business operations and gain a deep understanding of your customers and the market, which will help you make better decisions. On top of that, you will be less likely to waste your money on useless operations that are not critical to the success of your business.

It might be challenging to invest a lot of time in your new business, especially if you are working a 9-5 job and want to build your business on the side. However, the beauty of starting a drop shipping business is that it's easier to run on a part-time basis than running a brick-and-mortar business. All you need are a few hours a day or about 10 to 15 hours a week. During these early days, most of your efforts should be focused on marketing your business. As your business starts growing and the money starts flowing in, you can gradually transition into working on it full-time.

When investing time in your drop shipping business, the other thing you should keep in mind is that in the early days, you may need to put in a lot of effort and see no real results. However, once your store is up and running, you will need significantly less time to maintain it, and you will start making more money while doing less work.

Investing Your Money

If it is impossible for you to dedicate time to your drop shipping business, you may be able to grow your business by investing a bunch of money in it. However, I don't advise that, and I will always insist that if you can, you should always be out there doing most of the work and getting your hands dirty. Without a hands-on approach to the business, you will only end up wasting your money on useless operations that will not drive the overall success of the business. However, it's important to note that even if you decide to work full-time on your new business, you will still need some capital to launch the business and get operational.

Register Your Drop shipping Business

Remember that your business has to be legally registered with proper government agencies before you can start working with drop shipping suppliers. When it comes to registering businesses in the United States, three business structures are commonly used:

Sole proprietorship: This is the simplest structure you can register your business under. It has minimal filings, and your business earnings can simply be reported on your personal taxes. However, this structure offers no liability protection, which means that if your business is sued, your personal assets will also be at risk.

Limited Liability Company (LLC): This structure establishes your business as a separate legal entity, thereby providing more protection for personal assets. While an LLC offers more protection than a sole proprietorship, the protection is not foolproof. An LLC will also come with additional filing requirements.

C Corporation: C Corporations provide the most liability protection. However, registering and incorporating a C Corporation is more expensive than the other two. C Corporations are also subject to double taxation.

As a small entrepreneur, you should probably register your business as a sole proprietorship or an LLC. Personally, I feel that an LLC is the best choice for a drop shipping business. However, I would recommend that you consult with a lawyer before making a final decision on this.

After you register your business, you should then apply for an Employer Identification Number (EIN). This number is like the Social Security Number of your company. You will need to provide this number when applying for a wholesale account with your drop shipping supplier. You will also use it to file your taxes and do other official matters related to your business. You can apply for your business EIN online.

The other thing you need to do is make sure that you keep your business and personal finances separate. Blending your personal and business finances will cause confusion, make accounting a nightmare and may even get you into trouble with the IRS. The best thing is to ensure you keep the two totally separate. To do this, you should set up a separate bank account for your business, get a separate credit card, and create a separate PayPal account for your business.

Chapter 7 The Advantages of Retail Arbitrage

The thresholding for startup costs is quite low in this day and age, unlike any other retail business. And of the great parts about it is that there are companies that support other companies and their selling and drop shipping businesses. It is relatively simple to jump into this stream and sell on sites without even a subscription fee. The companies that support other drop-shippers will receive a cut from the profits but they will be in good standing with these companies, like for example, Amazon. Companies like Amazon help other businesses progress through their business expanding, also considering high web traffic and high buyer rates. The great reputations will be a great base for the distributors with their shops of retail arbitrage flowing and it will also be a great reputation to uphold. Orders are going to be fulfilled properly for every customer and they will have to meet a certain standard to be processed and shipped. We haven't talked about the product yet so we have to consider manufacturers when we consider using these extra sources to help us create product revenue. Retail arbitrage can be easier when used through a system and through a formula.

There have to be healthy ROI rates in order for them to carry over profits for the company. Mind this that ROI and net profit are two different worlds and you cannot call these two the same thing. On FBA sites that assist companies in their dropshipping, duties often have rules and fees. Items that typically sell for anything less than $20 will usually have fees of $4.01, which will also be a package that is under 2 pounds. Then you must add the 15% fee or $3 for the $20 dollar item that is being listed, which if that item cost you only $10 dollars, then through the purchase, the company will have made a margin of 2.99 and the ROI of this would be 30%.

There has to be a reasonable balance between purchases by volume and by margin because there are going to be markets to hold for consistent sales. Some sales are going to be supplied through means of a high volume of buyers visiting the source for many common goods or necessities perhaps, or there is going to be sales driven by marginal profits made to keep sales from wavering and a constant stream of buyer traffic to the shop. The company needs to keep a steady stream of incoming traffic for there to be strong numbers through the profits. The fees will help the profit breakeven for every purchase as long as there is a good price set for the product. There can be a gray zone for the price zone and it can make or break the company's chances of getting the sale over another company that has the same products. This is going to come when the company is deciding on what products to purchase and having a stable sourcing supplier that is going to be dedicated through their selling adventures. Depending on the size and the weight of the product that is being shipped, these FBA policies are going to apply under different rates and charge accordingly on a fixed process. It may be efficient to have a product that is a good proportionate weight to the price point of the product and otherwise will cut into the listing price, which could also result in higher profits earned. This should be strategically handled with a formula that is meant for handling profit revenue and marginal income for the shop. With arbitrage restocking, certain shelves for products is going to come with its setbacks if the company is selling a product that is not popular, but once the company takes a deeper dive into spending more money on better quality items, they are going to find it easier to sell in massive quantities and make consistent sales from selling the same items. There is an important niche to go with the trends at times, but other times it is going to be profitable to sell the same items once the company recognized the impact it is making to their monthly revenue. Find the right product to sell and it will make the fees and regulations easier to abide by with these selling systems. There needs to be an economic standpoint taken when considering what the right product will be when you are selling these items, and that is why companies like Amazon through FBA give lists of several products to choose from. These products range from home décor to auto shop appliances, and there could be many avenues taken as the suppliers are ready to stock by the thousands.

Budget Dynamics

Through basic retail arbitrage, the company will be able to list products at a marked down cost and make a great profit off of distinctive sales made on other platforms through different means. These sale strategies could range anywhere from personal investment sales that could be exclusive or to other distributors or companies that are trying to get a better deal on their bulk buying. There are budget dynamics that need to be made at the beginning of the purchases and all profits need to be formulated before there is a leap of money to be dropped on new inventories. These budget dynamics are going to be formulated depending on the current product that is being distributed and at what rate there will be selling these products. To list more products, it could be an extra charge for the space in the market and this will also have to be a factor to think about if the company is selling one thousand items or even ten thousand items. Keep a good track of every dollar spent and make sure it is going to the right accounts for the right purposes.

Need Low Budget for Starters

There is going to be a great entry budget for selling retail arbitrage considering that you can generate revenue with a good product that can make you consistent income to maintain revenue growth. A company can start gaining profits with a $300 budget and they will be able to make more moves with their startup costs. If the company is purchasing 100 pieces of inventory to flip for their customers, then the profits they receive from these units will be able to generate revenue for the company to then get 150 units for the next quarter. This will increase until the company has reached 1000% capacity of their original inventory plane. Once the company begins to sell 1000 units and then 1500 units of the inventory, the company will begin to receive extra revenues and dividends for the extra inventory that is making its way to racking up on the online shelves. Extra inventory is going to lead to extra sales and special events.

Easy to Get Started

This is an easy process to get going as long as there are an initial money budget and a general focus to where the company's motives are going to be made. The company is going to need to do product research and have a firm grasp of their product market and what crowds are going to be sold to for maximum exposure. The company may have to expand on other products or begin drop shipping other products if there is a change in the trending topics, or if the product takes revenue cuts through production manifesting. There is going to be a lot of hard work initially for these works, and it is necessary to find oneself going the extra miles to satisfy the customers that are being drop-shipped to. Branching out to find new clients is going to be a crucial part of finding a great niche in the scene that has dedicated buyers. Find a great product that isn't going to be falling off of the sales graphs any time soon, and if it is a common good, then there can be a continuous fan base built on the same values. Online shoppers everywhere are looking for fast and convenient shipping which is a great pride Amazon can take part in. Amazon offers a lot of perks to not only their customers but the businesses that are scaling up with them. Through Amazon fulfillment services, companies are able to meet high standards by shipping and handling high product loads for customers that are in need around the world. They take out the huge stress of managing inventory and create simple means to get products to the customers. With these services, it gives everyone a chance to become a part of the revolutionizing change in e-commerce. Anyone can use these services whether they are selling goods every day for a living, or if they are leaving college and trying to get rid of extra things that can be marked down. OA is already going to be marked down so the simplicity of creating profits from sourced items is going to be easy once the right formula for ROI and price count is established.

Easy to Scale-Up

Scaling up with retail arbitrage is going to be determined on the amount of drive and money that is put into the shops reach. There is going to be a possible gate on the amount of inventory that needs to be purchased, but as long as the company scales up with the products and proportions that are manageable to the company, the structure will be figured in a strong manner. There needs to be a threshold made between the number of products that are being purchased and the annual ROI, which can keep good standing with the margins that are earned every quarter. Lower ROI is going to create great progress for any company that is trying to make a set goal of profit in a fixed amount of time. Other processes can be made by purchasing many different products with different ROI's, and this is going to create a more diverse profit field which could be more high-end.

Chapter 8 How to Pick the Right Products

The biggest challenge you'll face when you start out as a retailer considering drop shipping is deciding what niche and products to sell. Not surprising, considering that this decision will be the biggest one you make and can make or break your business.

A lot of people make the most basic mistake while deciding. They go for what they are passionate about or are interested in. This is fine if you're more interested in selling a particular product or catering to a particular niche and profits aren't really a concern. But if you want to turn your business into a profitable enterprise, you'll need to do extensive market research on the viability of selling that product or even discard your personal preferences when making such a decision.

Here are some criteria that you'll need to keep in mind when deciding upon your niche and products.

Questions You Need to Ask Before Choosing Any Product

The wide array of products you will see will be enough to confuse you about everything that you could ever need and what you should purchase. You can make it less complicated by asking yourself the following questions:

How much risk am I willing to take?

Do you want to sell high ticket items? Those that are expensive may be harder to sell because of course, not everyone has the money every day to purchase those items. At the same time, the risk may be greater for you if the product would turn out to be defective or problematic. Just remember that if you do decide to take higher priced items, they can also give higher rewards.

Who is my target market?

Who is the market that you are trying to reach? Are you trying to be appealing to the younger market? Perhaps you would like to sell clothing items and accessories that they will find appealing. Once you get to know your target market, it will be easier to make choices about the items that will appeal to them in general.

Are the products easy to search?

The easier the products are to search, the higher the chances that people are searching for those different products online. Of course, if there are a lot of people searching for those items, this is enough reason for you to start selling those items on your website.

How to Sell Online Successfully

If you want your e-commerce business to thrive, you'll need to take one of the following paths.

Manufacturer – If you make your own product and sell it, you are in control of the distribution, and you may be the only source for that product. The advantage here is that you may not face a lot of competition and you can charge a higher price. However, if you want to go the way of drop shipping, this isn't a viable option.

Get Access to Select Distribution or Pricing – One way you can sell online and make a profit without having to manufacture your own product is by having an arrangement with the manufacturer that either lets you exclusively sell the product or gives you access to select pricing. Such arrangements, however, aren't easy to get into. In addition, there are plenty of other drop ship retailers who'll sell similar products and do so at wholesale prices.

Charges the Lowest Price – The most obvious advantage here is that you'll be able to take business away from a lot of your competitors. The reason that it isn't tried very often is that such a business model almost never works. If a low price is all you have to offer to your customers in terms of value, then you'll start a pricing war that will remove pretty much any profit margin you might have. It's not a good idea to compete with online giants such as Amazon based solely on price.

Adds Additional Value by Offering Information – This is the most effective ways to set you apart from the competition and charge a first-rate price. The whole point of entrepreneurship is that you solve problems that people have. This doesn't change when you decide to go the way of drop shipping. If you want your retail enterprise based on drop shipping to work out, the best way to make sure it does is to offer specialist guidance and advice. So the next question that you'll ask is how you can add value.

How to Add Value in e-Commerce

Now this is a part that's not quite that easy. There are niches and products in which you can add value quite easily. Then there are others that aren't quite as easy to work with. When trying to do this look for some traits that make it easier for you to add value with content that educates and guides. You need to search for niches and products that:

Have a lot of components – This one is actually quite simple when you think about it. If a product has a lot of components, people are going to go online to figure it out. Buying an office chair is less confusing than buying a DSLR camera with the attendant lenses and other components. It's obvious that if a product needs a lot of components and if those components are quite varied, you have a better chance to add value by letting customers know what products are compatible.

Are confusing or customizable – As Similar to the previous criterion, products that can be customized or require plenty of directions are perfect when you want to add value. If you can offer detailed advice on how certain products fit into different situations, which options are best for them and what product suits what customer, you can add tremendous value.

Need Technical Installation or Setup – Products that are complicated in terms of how they are meant to be installed or set up provide excellent opportunities for you to add value. For example, if you're selling music systems for cars, and you also sell a 40 page guide on how to install the system, what mistakes not to make installing it, how to sync it to your cell phone and so on, people are going to buy the guide from you at the same time as they buy the system to avoid the hassle of having to figure the whole thing out for themselves. Once such guides have been made, you don't have to pay anything to provide them to the customers.

Things You Need to Consider When Deciding Upon the Product

The Best Price – When deciding whether to sell lower or higher-priced products, you will want to consider the level of pre-sale service you can provide. If a customer is going to spend around $150 on a product online, he or she is more likely to buy it without needing to talk to someone on the phone about it. However, if the customer is looking a product priced at $1800, especially one that they don't know much about, they're more likely to want to talk to a sales representative so they can ensure that they're buying something that works for them and that the store is genuine.

If you do decide to go the way of high-priced products, you'll need to ensure two things: that you can provide the level of pre-sale services your customers will expect and that providing such service doesn't eat away into your profit margin. It is a good reason to consider products that range between $100 and $200 since they don't require a lot of pre-sale services.

MAP Pricing – There are manufacturers who set a minimum advertised price (MAP) for the goods they manufacture. In such a case, resellers need to price these products at a specific level or above it, as per the manufacturer. This helps to control price wars that can break out for products that are drop shipped easily. In turn, it also ensures that resellers make a decent profit when they sell that manufacturer's products.

Look for a niche where the manufacturer has enforced MAP pricing. This can be to your advantage, especially if you plan to add value to a site that is high-value and has a wealth of information. Since prices won't be very different from the competition, you won't be competing based on price and instead can compete based on your website, which ensures that you don't lose out to the lower-quality but cheaper competition.

Marketing Potential – You need to plan out your marketing before you begin, not once you've started and then realized that you're having trouble getting customers. Is there a way to promote your store by giving out some products for free or getting in touch with online communities that use the product you sell or even writing articles? If not, then don't consider this niche.

Plenty of Accessories – In general, in the world of retail, margins on higher-priced products aren't nearly as high as those on lower-priced products. For example, although a store that sells televisions may only make a 10% margin on the latest smart TV, it will make a margin of about 100% to 200% on the cables that go with it.

Think about it. When you go to purchase a high-priced item, you're much more careful about how much you end up paying for it. You'll probably shop around for the best smart TV at best possible price. But who shops around for the cables? You don't go from store to store trying to find the best price on something that may cost you about $50 to $60 dollars. You'll probably end up buying it from the store that you bought the TV from.

Low Turnover – By now it should be clear that you will get profits if you go for a good quality site that is rich in information. However, if what you've decided to sell is something that changes or gets updated every year, maintaining such a site will mean a lot of work for you. It is better to invest in products that don't get updated frequently or even every year. This means that the time, money and effort you spend on creating a good site lasts much longer.

Not Easily Available Locally – Your chances of success increase if you're able to identify and sell products that aren't easily available locally but don't get too specific with them. If someone needs a hammer or a garden rake, they're going to check out the neighborhood hardware store. But if you're looking for a falcon training kit or a medieval knight's costume, that isn't so easy. Most people go straight to Google and begin searches.

In Most Cases, Smaller is Better – This is the world of free shipping. Because of this, you may find it difficult to sell large and heavy products that are expensive to ship. Smaller items are easy to ship inexpensively.

While these factors are important, there are two other factors that can trump everything on this list.

Product Demand – Your product may qualify at 100% on the traits I've listed, but you still won't make any money or sell anything if there is no demand for it. You're better off trying to fulfill an existing demand than trying to create a new one. Tools such as Google Keyword Tool and Google Trends can help you identify what the demand for your product is based on search volumes, locations, and search volumes over time, most popular search queries, seasonality and geographic concentration of demand.

Competition – This part can be a bit tricky. If you face too much competition in a particular niche, you could get lost in all the noise out there. However, if you have very little competition, it could mean that there isn't much demand for that niche. While some drop shipping stores do rely on paid advertising, most of them depend on free traffic from search engines. That means that when you research your competition, you need to focus on the sites that come up on the first search page of Google and not the paid ones. When doing this, keep these metrics in mind: a number of linking domains, competing for sites' authority, site usefulness and quality and customer loyalty and site reputation.

Should You Sell Something You Genuinely Like?

There are some people who understand that in order for the items to sell, they need to focus on what the customers want but is this truly the case? Are the customers only the ones that need to be considered? You may want to consider what you want too.

You had started this business because you would like to have the opportunity to build a better future for yourself and probably your family but before you started, what were you doing? Do you consider yourself to be passionate about reading? Perhaps you have always considered decorating to be your strongest skill. You will always have some passions that you can easily incorporate into your business.

When you consider your passion, you find other products to sell that you genuinely want people to see. For example, if you have always loved art but lamented the lack of items that can be used by professionals for their artwork, then you can be the first drop shipping company to find suppliers that can give the type of art products that people are searching for. This will help your site become easier to recognize and appreciate by different individuals.

At the same time, this will allow you to see if there is an opportunity that was not explored yet. When you begin to offer something to the public that they have never seen or experienced before, you will be recognized for it. Even if other drop shipping companies start offering what you are selling, you will have an advantage because you were the first one who started selling it.

A Few More Things to Taking into Consideration

- If you are going to sell items that have copyright logos, (shirts, books, and other items) you need to make sure that you have gotten the approval of the company that owns the copyright to these products. A case may be filed against you if you are not an authorized seller. It can even be harder if you are selling fakes so try to stay away from counterfeit items.

- Start small with your product selections. It is okay to be passionate about what you are doing and to wish to compete with big brands someday eventually but if you cannot do it yet, then accept this first. The time will come when you will be one of the most successful ones, but as of now, you can practice humility and stay within your range.

- Items that are fragile are always riskier. Let us say that you have always loved ceramics and you know other people who would appreciate if you would sell ceramics as well, but these products come with a higher risk as compared to plastic products that can be sold easily. Consider the pros and cons of each item before deciding if you would offer that item or not.

Top Products Usually Sold in Dropshipping

In case you are still not sure about the variety of products that you are going to sell, here are just a few things that you can add to your line up. Just remember that you are still encouraged to pick depending on your target market.

1. Beauty Products

You can expect that this is something that people will always need. A lot of women are always on the lookout for beauty products that they can use depending on the occasion. For example, they may need a complete set of eye shadow that will allow them to do a smoky eye makeup. They will purchase different ones available.

2. Clothing

The thing about clothing is that they are always in demand. As long as you would have the right pieces of clothing to sell, you know that you are going to make a profit. Buyers can purchase a single item, but there are times when they would purchase an entire wardrobe from you. This can do a lot of wonders to your sales.

3. Accessories

Accessories are also other things that are always in demand. As long as you have the right accessories to sell depending on the season, you will be able to sell things and make some profit.

4. Smart Phones

Aside from smart phones, you can sell the usual bar phones if people would want something simple. People are always on the lookout for cell phones that do not cost a lot of money and if you can offer that through your website and you can prove that you will be able to provide good quality smartphones then you have nothing to worry about. The best thing about selling cell phones is that you can sell different ones created by various manufacturers. You are not limited to just one brand so let people explore the options you can offer.

5. Books

Although not everyone can appreciate reading, this is one category that is immensely popular with online shoppers. If you want, you have the option also to sell products that are used. You can search for suppliers that can offer titles that are hard to find and for sure, a lot of bookworms will start checking out your site for the newest titles you can offer.

6. Toys

This is once again, another category that is always appreciated. There are a lot of kids who would enjoy getting a toy, especially during special occasions. Having a nice selection of toys will allow buyers to purchase from your drop shipping website. Just make sure that you will double check all of the toys that you sell so they are all safe to use.

7. Furniture

One of the main problems of people, whenever they are purchasing items, is that they have to consider the shipping of the item from the furniture store where they have bought the item. Some people do not like the fact that they have to check the furniture from the actual store and then wait for it to be shipped. Through drop shipping, the item can be picked online, and it will be shipped depending on your rates.

8. Computer Related Accessories

At this day and age, there are still a lot of people who use computers because it cannot be denied that they are still a strong product that is worth having. You know that you need your computer for your business and there is a big possibility that people use computers for their various purposes as well. Selling accessories that will make computers easier to use can be best sellers.

Other Options

Let us say that you do not want to rely too much on suppliers. What can you do then? If this is the case, the best thing that you can do is to sell your own items. Of course, this takes away the element of drop shipping so if you do this, it will be like you are starting your own online business and you are not starting your very own drop shipping business.

Having the Best Customers

Depending on the products that you are going to sell, you are going to have different customers available. Remember that not all customers are the same. There are some who tend to feel entitled because they have purchased something even if it is just a little trinket and even if the item does not have real value at all.

What you should do is make sure that you will sell the right products so you can attract the right customers to check out your drop shipping company's website. Here are some of the customers that you should attract:

1. Other businesses - You can expect that business owners are going to buy a lot of items from your website. If you are able to build your relationship

with them and eventually get their trust, you know that you will be able to work with them for quite a long time.

2. Recurring Buyers - You will have some customers who will buy from you often. Whenever they need something, they know that your site is the best option that they have. Having returning customers is always fulfilling because this means that you are slowly building the number of customers who trust your website and your company.

3. People who have different hobbies - It can be fun to cater to hobbyists because you know that there are always different things that they would like to try and build. You can sell different tools that can cater to various hobbies like woodworking, embroidery, etc.

Chapter 9 Find a supplier

The next step is to find a company with which we can collaborate. What kind of collaboration are we looking for? The company must produce or purchase the goods we want to sell, and send them to our place for those who buy them from us.

Before starting to suggest how and where to look for companies of this type, it is appropriate to make a digression on the importance of the geographical location of this partner with whom we are launching.

It is no secret that a large quantity of products are made in East Asian countries, especially China. I will then refer to a Chinese supplier, but the same reasoning will be applied to any company with warehouses in Asia, America and generally outside the US.

It is definitely easier to find a Chinese supplier for the products we want to sell, and in many cases it is a good solution.

The first point in favor of a collaboration with a Chinese company is therefore the ease in contacting and starting a collaboration. There are portals used for this purpose, which we will discuss later, which simply allow us to search for companies based on the products they sell.

This point is important not only to start our business quickly, but also to ensure continuity in case of problems with a supplier: it will be very easy to find a new supplier in China, while it is much more difficult to find one in the US.

Another advantage of working with a Chinese partner is the price. As you can guess, the Chinese supplier is much closer than a community supplier at the beginning of the distribution chain and can afford to sell at prices that may seem, at first glance, incredibly advantageous.

It is important, in this case, also to consider the costs of managing and shipping orders, but in principle it is correct to say that a Chinese supplier has decidedly costly costs.

The practice of drop shipping from China is very common, so when you talk about drop shipping to your potential supplier, this will probably immediately understand what you mean and what kind of collaboration you are asking. Despite the time zone difference and the language barrier, English is a must, communication is often effective and it is generally easy to maintain good working relationships.

To be taken into consideration are, however, also against the purchase from a Chinese supplier or in general, from an extra-US supplier: the first of all are shipping times.

Economic shipments from China require weeks for delivery, and it is not uncommon for an order made today to be delivered a month or more later. This is a problem because often customers are impatient to receive the products, and a long delivery time will lead to bad moods, as well as considerably increase the number of contacts to customer service, requests that will also be managed. It is imperative to declare in advance what are the shipping times of the goods, but it is not always sufficient to prevent these episodes.

A second disadvantage to consider is customs costs. As the goods arrive directly from the supplier to the consumer, the consumer himself will be responsible for customs duties if these are foreseen. Recall that it is necessary to specify it clearly so that the customer knows, before the purchase, that it could be subject to additional charges. Our business can offer to fully repay these expenses, going to affect our margin. The problem of customs is presented, however, only for objects that have an initial value above a certain community threshold, set at 22 euros.

The drop-shipper, who is then to sell items of value below this threshold, will not have to worry in any way of the customs problem since every single import will be exempt. If, instead, there should be goods of a higher value it is advisable to inform the customer.

If the points in favor of an extra-US supplier win on the other hand, it will only be the entrepreneur who decides it, according to the specific situation.

The search for a Chinese supplier is very simple, thanks to the existence of online portals that act as a showcase.

One of the fastest ways to find a supplier is to search on Ali-Express. Ali-Express is a website very similar to Amazon, where Chinese sellers can sell their items directly to the end customer. However, it is little known outside of China, so it is a great place to start looking for our suppliers. Once found on Ali-Express, we can agree with the seller to find a way to collaborate; but even if not, we will be able to buy the goods we sell on Ali-Express, to send them directly to our customer!

With Ali-Express it is, therefore, possible to have a large number of automated suppliers, who do not even know how to sell to another company, because they are asked to send directly to our customer.

We could instead consider looking for a fixed supplier with whom to undertake a more stable and lasting working relationship.

Also in this case we can contact our supplier on Ali-Express and explain him our need.

For the direct search for a supplier of this type, the website I recommend is the famous Alibaba, a sort of online showcase of Chinese suppliers, wholesalers and producers.

On Alibaba, it is not obvious that we will find who will accept to ship with the drop shipping method, it will be necessary to do several searches and contact several companies before finding one with which to collaborate. But with greater effort, better results are often obtained, and in fact, a direct partnership with a supplier certainly has several advantages compared to the direct purchase through Ali-Express:

- Prices will be more profitable, especially if we can show the supplier what our sales capabilities are

- It will be possible to personalize the unboxing experience, even if only with business cards with the brand of our store, if we do not want to invest in customized packages or products

- We will always be in contact with an expert supplier in the field, who will have an interest in keeping us updated on new products

Despite these important advantages, the convenience of searching for a product on Ali-Express is not to be underestimated, so much so that in several adventures I started selling products with the Ali-Express method, and then going to a supplier of Alibaba only at a later time.

Other portals to find suppliers using the Ali-Express method, that is, retailers to send directly to our customers, are Deal-Extreme, Light-In-The-Box, Bang-good and Gear-best; as an alternative to Alibaba we find Global-Sources instead.

As we have seen, it is very easy to find suppliers in China. The opposite is unfortunately true for US suppliers.

In fact, despite the advantages in the speed of shipping and communication, it is extremely rare to find a US supplier that accepts drop shipping and at the same time provides convenient prices.

Some of the suppliers I worked with are Big-Buy and Italian WWT, while others can be found through You-Droop and E-sources.

Finally, let's not forget that, as with Ali-Express, we could order products from retailers, the same we can do now. We always look for the product also on Amazon and eBay, and we could find cheap prices!

A last possibility is that of Chinese traders with warehouse in the USA. Some of the websites mentioned above, such as Gear-best or Deal-Extreme, have American stores from which you can order with a minimum surcharge.

Availability is not huge, but if we have the opportunity to sell products in this way, we can combine the advantages of a Chinese supplier with a national shipment!

How to submit orders
In order to optimize our resources as much as possible, it is necessary, as far as possible, to automate the procedure for sending the order from our shop to our supplier.

If we decide to work with Ali-Express, we can use a Shopify application called Oberlo.

Oberlo allows you to connect our products to those in the Ali-Express store, or even to import the products directly from our store.

Finally, Oberlo has an extension of the Google Chrome browser that allows you to automate the procedure of placing orders: simply access the Oberlo orders panel and press the "Fulfill Order" button to watch the extension work in our place!

Other websites, such as Bang-good and Deal-Extreme, offer special discounts and different conditions for partners who sell their products in dropshipping, so I recommend always check directly on the supplier's website for special benefits.

If we find a company with which we can collaborate directly. For example, how we can do on Alibaba, it will be necessary to find an agreement on how to submit the orders. Some ideas can be:

- Export orders in CSV or Excel format from Shopify, and forward these files to the supplier. He will then have to respond by providing the tracking codes of the goods shipped.

- Forward the order confirmation e-mails to the supplier, to every purchase that our store receives. This feature can be set directly on Shopify.

- Provide the supplier with a manager account of our e-commerce, so that he can log in, check the orders and mark them as shipped.

Chapter 10 Contacting Suppliers

This chapter focuses on supplier drop shipping because retail arbitrage, etc., doesn't require any license or anything because you're just a consumer.

Once you've found your suppliers, it's time to contact them. Suppliers usually don't have much time, so you need to have a few things to reassure them that you're not jerking them around, otherwise you're going to be wasting your own time.

The very first thing you should do is get yourself an actual company, whether it be a corporation or limited liability. Name it something appropriate, and apply for it in your state/country. It's very cheap and quick to do this with applications only costing $50 in some states. This is one of the main things that I find people are scared of; just a simple company that will protect you if anything goes wrong, but everyone thinks you need some sort of legal lawyer to file it all for you with heaps of paperwork.

This also means to create a company bank account, because it just makes your life far easier. By that, I mean, with so many incoming and outgoing transactions, using a personal bank account is going to make accounting extremely difficult by any means, so you have to make sure you're organized or you're not going to be an efficient and effective business. This will save you money because your accountant won't need to comb through hours of personal stuff, and only focus on the business stuff.

You also need to think about what you want. If you want couches, you need to make sure you say that. Don't contact a supplier asking them what they sell, because their catalogues are usually huge and they won't bother with you if you haven't already done your homework on them.

Once you are organized, you should contact your supplier either by email, phone or real life. Although I've said trade events and all that aren't useful for me, if you know what you're going after and know what you need from them, they'll be willing to listen. Real life is probably the best, since you're creating a personal and business relationship, so you're doing two things at once. But email and phone aren't bad either, and, if you're one of those introverts who has no confidence on the phone, you're going to have to man up, because a lot of suppliers will follow up via phone to confirm things, such as banking information.

I always recommend emailing, then following up via phone if you get no response. But you should be straight up with the supplier and just ask if they provide to double check. You will then be asked if you're interested in their drop shipping program and fill out a form for your online store. Sometimes, a lot of these suppliers will want proof that you're already bringing in traffic so you're not jerking them around.

When they've verified your store and all that stuff, they'll ask you for your account and other personal details. The process is pretty much self-explanatory. It'll likely take a week to deal with all this, sometimes more if need be, but you don't want to get this part wrong, and neither does your supplier.

Whenever choosing a payment method with your supplier, I prefer to just use an end of month payment method. It's much simpler for accounting purposes, and, if you're a bit OCD, seeing many different transactions makes you a little sick. The other methods are credit card, wire and check (which you'll send at the end of the month).

Overall, contacting suppliers is obviously very important, so get it right. Never ask for their catalogue because they're huge and you don't have the time to waste time. Just re-read this chapter before you actually contact a supplier.

Chapter 11 All about Orders

Orders with drop shipping happen differently from traditional e-Commerce orders because the retailer selling the products has nothing to do with the products themselves. Despite this fact, it is still important that you understand the order process and the role that you play in it, in order that you know how you can contribute to successful ordering experiences for your customers. This will also help you know what to do should any troubles arise, so that you are taking all of the necessary actions to offset these risks and develop your business.

In this chapter, we are going to discuss everything about orders, ranging from how to deal with them and what to do should any troubles arise during the ordering process.

Security

Creating a secure purchasing experience for your customers is crucial for them, as well as for you. In this day and age, people will rarely purchase online unless they feel confident that their purchases are going to be safe and that they are not investing their money into a scam. Improving security with your business by creating a secure checkout process for your customers is vital. The best way that you can improve order security is by using a strong platform like Amazon, Shopify, Big-Commerce, Woo-Commerce, or any other well-known platform that can offer a strong checkout process. Refrain from using any unknown platform or one that seems to lack strong ratings, as this could result in your checkout process not being nearly as secure. Stick to well-known names so that your customers feel confident and safe when purchasing with you.

Fraud Issues

Using a well-known point of sale platform is a great way to eliminate fraud issues within your business. Ideally, you want to use a platform that is going to protect both yourself and your customers from possible fraud so that everyone feels safe as they use the checkout process. One big type of fraud that drop-shippers face is credit card fraud, where people will purchase products through them with a credit card, and then order a chargeback through their credit card company to receive the funds back. This results in them having to pay for the product that the individual received, and the individual receiving a refund for that product. In other words, they end up getting the product for free, and in many cases, they will go on to sell the product so that they can earn the profit from it instead.

Protecting your company from credit card fraud starts with using a company like Amazon or Shopify which has built-in features that are meant to protect merchants like you against this type of fraud. In these cases, certain shipping labels are used, which prove that the product was delivered, making it more challenging for the individual to request a chargeback.

Another thing you can do to look out for possible cases of fraud is to check for common red flags that indicate that fraud could be taking place. For credit card fraud, the common signs include an individual who has different billing and shipping addresses, different names, strange emails that appear to be fake, rush shipping especially on expensive purchases, package re-routing, or unusually large orders. All of these behaviors are common behaviors that take place when credit card fraud is happening, and can massively impact your business. If you notice any suspicious behaviors like this taking place, you can take action to prevent the sale from going through with your company.

One great way that you can minimize fraud and prevent chargebacks is by using a managed services solution, which is a company that pays attention to your incoming orders to prevent the risk of fraud. As your company grows, this may be an ideal opportunity for you to avoid being put at risk of these forms of fraud. A great company to consider should you want to use a service like this is Clear-Sale, which has built-in features that monitor your orders and flag possible fraudulent orders to prevent them from going through.

Product Returns

Strict return policy can prevent you from having to deal with returns or refunds, but it can also drive people away from doing business with you since they cannot effectively test out your products to guarantee that they like them. If your return and refund policy are too strict, customers may not want to purchase from you because they will worry that if they have a problem, they cannot receive any support with the problem they have faced. Instead, they will go elsewhere to another business that has a better return or refund policy to purchase the same products.

Managing product returns and refunds with drop shipping can get messy, especially because the product has already been purchased from the wholesaler, which makes it more challenging for you to manage it. With dropshipping, you are dealing with the wholesaler's return policy, which means that if they have a strict return policy, you may have to refund the product and take it into your own possession, which begs the question: what then?

The best way to create strong return policies for your business is to choose suppliers who also have decent return policies, so that you can return the product directly to the supplier. Alternatively, you can use a company like Amazon FBA who completely manages all returns and refunds for you, and resells returned product to future customers. This way, rather than having returned products sitting in your own possession and with no way of really selling them, other than by selling them privately, they are all dealt with properly.

Shipping Issues

Running into shipping issues when you are a drop-shipper can be challenging. Some suppliers take days or even weeks to work through these problems, which can make it even more challenging for you to deal with them. If you, as a merchant, take too long to deal with shipping issues, it can become a huge problem for your business. The best way to deal with shipping issues is to pick a carrier and then use that same carrier for every single shipment. For example, you could use the U.S. Postal Service, or a shipping company like UPS or FedEx to do all of your shipping through. These services offer small businesses tools that they can use to calculate shipping on products, making it easier for those small businesses to offer consistent shipping rates. Alternatively, you could use Amazon FBA, which has its own shipping service that tends to be cheaper than going through your own private shipping deal with a company.

International Shipments

International shipments can be dealt with in the same way as domestic ones are, however, the pricing will be different. Offering a separate shipping option that provides prices for international customers is ideal to ensure that they are being charged for the entire shipping fee. This also ensures that you are not charging too much for the shipping fee, which could drive international customers away. Ideally, you should use the same carrier for international shipping that you use for domestic shipping, such that your shipping concerns are always easy for you to navigate.

Dealing with Out Of Stock Orders

Most of the suppliers that you work with are going to be supplying multiple drop shipping companies just like yours. This means that accidents can happen where the products they have to go out of stock and, on your website, it shows up as if they are still in stock. Unless you are using a company duo like Oberlo and Shopify, real-time updates are not often available, which implies that you could run into issues around this.

If a customer does order an out-of-stock product, the next best thing you can do is communicate with your supplier to determine when the product is going to be back in stock. If they are in stock quickly, you may be able to just let things go on as usual. Otherwise, it may be ideal to message that customer, offer an apology, and refund that part of their order. You may also consider offering them some form of an added bonus to make up for the inconvenience, such as free shipping on the rest of their order or a discount for their next purchase. In many cases, simply letting them know and offering a solution such as one of the ones previously mentioned will help you navigate these issues relatively seamlessly.

Inventory

While you run your drop shipping company, it is ideal to make sure that you have a system to help you identify how much stock is left in any given product, so that you can feel confident that you have plenty for your customers to order. If you use a simple company like Amazon FBA, this will be easy as Amazon updates your numbers on your dashboard to let you know how much stock you have left. Otherwise, you are going to have to regularly check in with your suppliers to see how inventory levels are going, in order that you know that there is plenty left for your customers to order. If you find that inventory levels with your supplier are low, you can always set a product to "out of stock" even before it officially goes out of stock to avoid running into this problem.

Dealing with orders in a drop shipping business can be somewhat tricky as you are more of a middle man than an actual retailer. Knowing how to manage orders and how to prevent fraudulent purchases, or other troubles from taking place during the ordering process, is important as this helps you prevent any issues from arising in your business. It is important that you educate yourself on all protocol around your orders with every single supplier that you use, in order that you know exactly what you need to do in the event of any form of order trouble. This way, everything can always be dealt with in a timely manner and without causing too significant troubles for you or anyone else involved in the ordering and order fulfillment process.

Chapter 12 Affiliate Marketing

Affiliate marketing is the most popular way of earning passive income. It is a way of earning through a commission by advertising and promoting other companies' (people) products and service.

You promote their products, so others can buy and then you earn a commission (part of the profit) for each sale made on the product resulting from your promotion. There are different ways of earning with affiliate marketing, but the most popular ways are;

- Creating an affiliate store

- Social Media

We will be looking into using Social Media to earn with affiliate marketing. Using Social Media can be one of the most effective ways of earning through affiliate marketing. Before we go into the detailed process of using affiliate marketing on Social Media, remember you will be doing this on your Social Media account, and you have contents that you post originally, DO NOT STRAY FROM THE CONTENT you post on your page. To start with, I'd recommend you partner with a company or brand that offers products or services relating to your businesses. If you have put a lot of effort into amassing active and well-engaged followers, squashing it all because of affiliate marketing is not worth it. I advise making at least 80% of your posts your own content and the remainder can be about promotions.

There are certainly tips that can be used for more effective affiliate marketing on Social Media.

- Excellent content: It might seem as if we have been so concerned about contents but as I said, the influencers say "content is the king". Ordinarily, the sight of anything related to affiliate marketing puts people off. The best and the first way to present it in a friendly way are by writing exceptional contents. You shouldn't depend on the affiliate links to describe the product, let your post do the talking. The power to attract the audience to the link you are pointing at is in your content, the destination link doesn't know your audience, and you know your audience. So only you have the words, skill, knowledge, and language to attract your audience. And don't write unnecessarily long content; keep it brief, concise and detailed.

- Be transparent: Honesty is the most powerful tool to employ in building a healthy, strong and lasting relationship with your audience. It helps them easily build their trust in you. Disclose your affiliation with your audience, when you do this, if they aren't interested, they'll just move on to something of interest to them. That's better than them stumbling on contents that surprisingly ministers disinterest.

- Make use of redirect links: Make use of redirect links: An affiliate link is another thing that put people off by mere seeing. A redirect link will be better, simpler, more friendly and attractive to click.

- Photos: Carefully select the pictures of products you promote, photos draw attention quicker than words. They are can be spotted easier than words or texts contents, when you are on a high-speed scroll; your eyes catch photos easily compared to texts. Use high-quality and attractive photos.

- Quality products: Don't just pick products at random, have a quality test for the products you are putting on your Social Media Page. If your audience is impressed by the quality of the purchase of the products they'll surely spread the word for you. That is better than just choosing products randomly; remember to choose "quality over quantity".

- Relate with other affiliate marketers: Relate with other affiliate marketers: There are different groups and forums of Affiliate Marketers that you can join online. Joining these groups will be very helpful for you, you will get to stay updated about what is trending in the affiliate marketing community as a whole, and you will get useful information that can make you improve your affiliate marketing skill.

- Sound natural: Do not make it sound like you are the salesperson, see and present yourself as someone who is just sharing a product or service that can be helpful to your audience. Keep your promotional tone low. If you want to promote a cloth washing machine, write something like "Do you find washing too much hassle? This washing machine might help." That is better and friendlier.

- Campaign analysis: You shouldn't just keep running your affiliate campaigns, analyze and optimize your campaigns so you'll know areas that need improvement if need be. And if your analysis shows that your campaign is failing, you will know how to quickly deal with the situation

- Research: Carry out good research on all the affiliate programs that you intend to sign up with. Know which one is going to probably work out well for you.

- Consistency: Retain your consistency, do not let affiliate marketing take away your engagement with your audience, and rather let it strengthen the bond. Your followers will ask questions about the products you post on your page, be sure to be available and ready to answer in time. It is still part of your business.

Now that you have known how to make use of your Social Media accounts to earn with affiliate marketing, let's discuss a few affiliate programs.

- Crowd fire: Crowd fire is a Social Media Marketing tool used all around the globe for Social Media management and growth. It can be used with Facebook, Twitter, YouTube, Instagram, pinterest, WordPress, and many other Social Media Platforms. Also, Crowd-fire is one of the biggest affiliate programs worldwide provides an affiliate program. They offer up to 35% commissions which can be as high as $400 per referred customer.

- Sendible: Sendible originally is a Social Media multipurpose tool that allows you to post scheduled updates, reply comments and create reports. They have an affiliate marketing which 30% recurring commission which can be up to $700 per client or customer.

- Social Pilot: Social Pilot is a Social Media automation tool that for automating posts. Their affiliate program yields up to 30% recurring commission.

- Commun.it: Commun.it as a tool is used to track brand mention, followers and lead on Social Media. Besides being a tool, they have a great affiliate marketing program with a 30% commission.

- Bluehost: Bluehost is a web hosting website; it was evaluated by some analytics to be the best web hosting we have today. Bluehost web hosting affiliate program is recorded to be one of the best affiliate programs that we have. They pay up to $60 - $130 per signup.

- Bigcommerce: This is a popular e-commerce platform for developing e-commerce websites. Their affiliate program is quite impressive. They pay a 200% commission depending on the plan which can be $60, 160$, $250 or $1,500 per paying customer.

- Trippayouts: This is a popular travel affiliate program that offers up to 80% commission.

The above are few affiliate programs in different fields that can be promoted through your social Media pages and can easily and passively earn you good income.

Affiliate Marketing is just a very interesting way of monetizing your audience on Social Media. But it is important that you keep your audience as your priority. Do not post anything to make them lose interest in you. Keep your Social Media Analysis tools handy, if you notice a drop in the number of your followers; quickly adjust the content you post. Nothing is worth you losing your followers.

Chapter 13 Running Your Own Dropshipping Business

In this chapter, we will look at some points to remember when running your own dropshipping business. By now, you should have a good idea what is behind running a drop shipping business and be aware of the main points and things you must do to get started. Before you dive straight in and begin dropshipping, it is worth considering a few important points that we will look at here.

It Takes Commitment

Having a dropshipping business can potentially make you a six-figure income; this isn't something rare and there are many success stories that prove this. How do you get this? You may have the most amazing product and incredible looking store, but to really lift this off and make money, you need to commit yourself to it both now, in the short-term future, and in the long-term. If you throw yourself into your business, then it's likely to be a success. If you half-heartedly update the store now and again and spend just a few hours a week on it, then it's unlikely to ever really grow. Remember, as an owner of a drop shipping business, you are a CEO and founder of that business and you have to start seeing yourself like that.

It Takes Time

You need to invest your time into your business to make it grow and this is especially true if you are entering the drop shipping world for the first time. You will have a lot to learn, including managing the store, how your business operates, and how to deal with demand when the business grows. You should take some time to get to know who your audience is and how you can appeal to them.

You may be working full-time right now so in the beginning it may be hard to juggle between the two jobs. But the result will be worth it as your business grows and you are able to be your own boss with control of your schedule and your profits. Even if you can dedicate just 10 or 15 hours a week to your drop shipping business, it is certainly possible to start earning between $1,000 and $2,000 per month after 12 months of being in business. Obviously, that can definitely increase with time if you keep channelling your effort and time into it.

The beauty about a drop shipping business is that after the first few months of dedicating your time and energy, once the business has kicked off, it takes less hours to maintain so eventually you will be earning a great income and working less hours. Not only that, but by building a successful business now, it is an asset for the future that can either continue to provide you an income stream or something you can sell.

It will be hard work in the beginning but the rewards are tremendous. You get to be your own boss, have flexibility over your schedule, can work anywhere in the world, and still earn a decent income. Once you have found success in one niche, you can easily branch out and start serving plenty of other niches and audiences and build your profits even more.

Let's recap over the process of starting you own drop shipping business and how to run it from that point.

The Entire Process of Setting Up And Running A Drop shipping Business

First things first, decide your niche by brainstorming ideas and seeing which one is most popular and profitable by first searching for related keywords in Google Keyword Planner and then checking to real-life popularity by searching the best keywords on platforms such as Amazon. You can also use social media sites such as Facebook, Reddit, and YouTube to see if there is a buzz about these keywords. After all this analysis, you can then decide which niche you want to work with.

Next, after picking products you want to sell in your niche, search for suppliers. You can either do this by searching specifically for drop ship suppliers in your niche and reaching out to them directly or you can use platforms such as Ali-Express, Alibaba, Sale-Hoo, or Doba that give you a whole marketplace of suppliers, manufacturers, and wholesalers.

Then, you want to start thinking about how your customers will know you exist. This is where marketing and branding step in. Think about your brand. What's its concept, what's its story? Develop this on social media, create a platform where your customers can see your product and communicate and interact with you directly. Nowadays, social media is one of the most important ways to reach customers for all businesses. Your brand should include a name (don't overthink this but pick something catchy and that you like), a logo, and a tagline. You can make a logo for just a couple of dollars on places like Fiverr and Up-Work.

Visit: fiverr.com

Visit: upwork.com

Next up is actually opening your store. You can set this up on whichever platform you prefer whether that's an open source platform or a hosted platform.

Then, start listing your products on your store, including images and detailed product descriptions. Now that you have your store, you know your niche, and you understand your brand better, you will have a good idea of what products will be best for you. You will need to speak with your supplier to get the best prices and make sure you understand all the important terms such as additional costs and delivery charges and times.

Make sure your site has product pages for your customers to find your products and also other important pages such as About Us, Contact Us, and FAQs. Having all of this from the beginning means that your site automatically has an air of authority and authenticity, which make help make new customers feel comfortable trusting you and buying from you.

Next, go ahead and start selling! Your site doesn't have to be totally perfect as you can iron out the details after. Just get the site out there so it can start doing its thing and earning you an income.

From then on, you can keep on making your site the way you want it and add more products. Keep your social media pages active and use them as a way of interacting and engaging with customers. How do you get these customers? Start by sharing your page with all your friends and family and encourage them to like and share your page too. Pay for Facebook ads and concentrate on building a blog with value-worthy content and a good SEO strategy to get your content found. Once you have success in one niche, expand to others while continuing to run the first one. Build your business and look for as many opportunities as possible that will help it grow, expand, and become more profitable.

Once your business is growing, you will need to streamline the order process as much as possible and start making your business efficient. Luckily, there are plenty of apps out there that you can use to make the interaction between your customers, your store, and your suppliers much easier and smoother. Some important ones include Oberlo (if you use suppliers through Ali-Express or in China), Klaviyo (an email marketing service, perfect to keep the communication with your customers), and Yotpo (helps add reviews in your store which is great to give customers some indication that they can trust you).

Visit: klaviyo.com

Visit: yotpo.com

These are just a few in a very large ocean of apps so look around and start adding them to your store. It will help make the business more professional and easier to manage.

Finally, you need to make sure you are analysing your business and constantly improving it. You need to check performance and enhance the things that are working and eliminate the things that aren't. How can you measure this? Two great tools are Google Analytics and Facebook Pixels which can show you where your customers are coming from, what's driving them to your site, and what's driving them away from your site too. Use this information to your advantage.

Follow these steps and you will have a successful drop shipping business. Thankfully, it's not magic. It's just knowing the right process, having the commitment and effort to make it work, and then actually going out there and doing it.

☐ A dropshipping business is a great way to be your own boss and earn a decent income. You just need to invest time and be committed.

☐ Remember, when you have a dropshipping business, consider yourself the CEO or the boss of your company. You are in charge and you can make it grow.

☐ To make and run a successful dropshipping business, you should follow a set of guidelines.

☐ First pick your niche and then find your suppliers. Then start thinking about your brand and once that's decided, open your store and list your products. Develop your site and start selling, all the while looking for ways to reach more customers and grow a larger audience. As your business grows, start streamlining its processes with apps and constantly analyse your data to look for ways to improve it.

Chapter 14 Scaling Up Your FBA Business

Scaling up the Amazon FBA business is not going to be a quick feat. This is not typically the case for businesses that are only making penny profits. There may have to be some product purchasing that gives the company an extra boost for quarterly profits. Usually, the company is going to pick from one to a few products to sell on the site. Purchase a great product that is going to be a money maker for the next coming quarters so that you can begin thinking of the next step. Once there has been enough revenue generation from the product that has been showing promising sales, keep flipping this product until there is a sum of money that is for investing further into the company. Use these gained profits to purchase more of the same product especially at a lower rate if you are purchasing into the next capacity brackets. If you do not want to purchase the same product, use some of the profits to purchase another product and list it to create a greater revenue flow. Now, products that sell are going to be helping each other keep a consistent profit rate.

Once you begin scaling up within Amazon FBA, there are going to be greater benefits with the service providers that are chosen to deal with these shipping deals. Amazon will give percentage points back on money spent on products that Amazon is listing and when the company sells these items, they will get them for a better price when they purchase in bulk. Once the company begins to ramp up, it will be good to optimize the products that are on the market. You can categorize the product differently, or place product ads to make an extended reach to certain buying crowds. Change up the product descriptions a bit to be more poppy for the consumer and watch the variations you make because some of them will bring in more buying traffic all because it is merely being optimized. A brand new look to the site can do some justice if things have been years before seeing a changeup, so don't be afraid to make new changes to the company that can promote new viewers to come. You can scale up the business by changing up the budget balance, and where most of the money made may have been going back into the inventory, we can think about new changes that can make a great difference to the flow. You are owning success in one category on Amazon, but how about creating two different product listings that can account for two different categories which can practically double the profits for the company. These are also going to be new learning curves for the company if they are diving into territory that has not been touched before. Finding great products to resell isn't always the easiest, but once you get the hang of it, you are going to have a hand in a few markets by the time you know it. Product choice is going to evolve as the company gets more exposure and as customers may begin to ask about different product variations, whether it be about other colors or other sizes and makes.

Methods for Obtaining Reviews

Create methods to obtain feedback from the fans and supporters of the e-commerce shop. There are tons of ways to get feedback from great individuals sharing their opinions about the product. Good and bad products alike will end up getting sometimes the truest opinions of the lot. Terrible products make consumers rant and give bad reviews for products, but these are often at times publicity stunts to gain some other type of revenue. Very good quality products are going to have the buyers rave about the purchase online, and this could be by having comments left on the page or by custom pictures being taken and left for others to see, and also judge the product by other visual enhancements. Pictures of the products on social media sites can also obtain reviews just by visual enhancement marketing tactics. Run a page that has your content on it and you will obtain followers. Invest time in a good marketing foundation that could be a separate firm running strong with the company, and they will handle all inbound traffic and possible leads. Reviews are great for those in the community that does not own the product yet. Now, think locally just on your site that means creating a comfortable atmosphere so that the consumers rate your shop good on the e-commerce platforms you decide to sell through.

Move into Wholesale

Merchants typically sell goods that are not purchased or selected in advance and before the products are sent to the consumers. Good products will bring sales and the customer orders leaving the consumer to price the product as they please. They purchase it at a wholesale value so it can have a high margin as long as you can still balance out a low ROI. Begin making connections with wholesaling companies that have products that are in your field. Pick a good product and the consumer will enjoy the variety when you present them with different costs for different qualities. It is going to be a ramp-up in price so mind that this step is going to require a bigger budget. Save up for this step so that you can purchase your first hundred units or five hundred units. These are stepping stones that are going to teach us the basics of OA. Good suppliers will give great prices when purchasing these quantities and when it gets into the thousands, it can really get to discount season. This is going to lead to a high yield for the consumer to place these new gains aside to save for their new steps. Let the product sell itself if you know it will. When visiting these wholesalers, look at how much they have shipped out before. Ask about their markets and who is typically buying or whatever curiosity you have and get to know your wholesaler.

Move into Private Labeling

Your Own Product
Some companies build revenue to brand their own products and this could be great for the overall marketing of the company. Labeling companies are doing business with thousands of sources right now that have an amazing number of products to choose from. Labeling companies work with any type of labeling designs or artistically enthused branding. When the company starts branding its own product, they will be able to have a customized product that is unlike any other. This product will be able to stand out and they will be able to design it to have a label or a box that shines. Generally, the white-labeled products aren't going to be the most original looking types of things because they are made in mass quantities. So it is necessary to go to external sources for possible artwork handling or logo designing that needs to be taken care of before this phase. Get creative with this step because there are going to be tons of competitors that are using the same methods as you. For all you know in the world of white labeling, the competitors could be using the same company as you for these services. Use this chance to create an unforgetful image for the customer to remember the product by. These private labeled companies are going to make it easy for consumers to diversify the product every quarter. Make ways to keep the product looking interesting

even if it means doing some boxing as well the same ways and make it clever and efficient to receive your packages.

Other's Products

When purchasing white-labeled products that are from other sources, the best part about that is going to be the price. There are great prices for locally made things that can be considered common goods and these goods can be purchased as well as wholesale and they can be flipped through OA. Avoid shipping costs to outlets and purchase locally to pick up with a truck or van. With these products, most customers do not know what the product actually is because it tends to be a plain form of a product that they are used to. These products may look like something they may know, but they could have no labels at all and just be a standalone product. This is okay if the product is high-quality, but the customer also relies on visual enhancements as we have spoken about in this book. Sell other products that are white-labeled to exclusive buyers and give good deals so that these buyers come back on a frequent basis. These products are best for buyers who are only looking for quantity and quality is typically the second concern. There are a lot of white-labeled great products out there and the quality just keeps getting better and better as the years of online shopping go on.

Advertise the Products

Marketing Firms

Marketing firms are a great way to get a product or a distributor a proper representation. Marketing firms are masters of the market and they can tap into most streams of public interest. These markets do anything from making phone calls to independent advertising that could be state to state by roadshows or other means of trade traveling. These firms hire good representatives that are well-established in their skills to be able to make online advertisements or ones of that in the retailer or at community areas as spokespeople. These opportunities usually come by advancements into the business markets all around. There can be special events made where companies make appearances by sponsorship and furthermore, these firms are going to be the perfect ones to go for to get it all organized. Marketing firms also generate other high forms of online traffic with their own servers, and this, in turn, is going to give you boosts to your traffic in buyers. A great team of marketers will charge for their services but it is quality effort to make sure that the company is being run to a certain degree of standards which can be designed to the company's needs. Marketing agencies create and establish a strategy which overall can conduct market survey research, and they can also build great relationships with your audience and increase exposure to the company, by engaging with potential customers that may be interested with the product you sell.

Telemarketing companies have a great hand in the marketing world. Companies like these have employees that make outbound phone calls to engage with future prospects and to take orders of any current. This is a vital role for any company that is handling a large quantity of shipments, considering that there is also a need for a customer service helpline established as well.

There are going to be digital marketing agencies that help improve the website, by advising to post or place social media accounts certain ways to market best to the viewers. Digital marketing can engage millions of customers around the world because they most likely are already on their device. Marketing firms tap in at the right time and also do extra promotions through the holiday times when it gets busier to keep up with the higher demand of traffic volumes.

Google Adwords

This tool is going to be vital if you are also using something like Google Ads. Google Adwords is a tool that acts a lot like a thesaurus which is a keyword identifier. Enter in the phrase you think your prospects are searching for in their browsers and Google will tell you similar phrases that may or may not relate. Google will tell the consumer how much a phrase is searched and how popular it will come to be in the end by the time someone buys it up. It is going to be costly for each keyword that is found, but it will really make the campaign boom if done properly with this tool. Use this tool if the company has not been named yet as a way to optimize the amount of traffic that can be earned through a different name.

Pay for Premium Accounts that Host Websites for Advertising

Paying for premium accounts is going to be a step when the company has had its time to adapt to the marketing world. This step is going to take more of the budget and it will be used to optimize more aspects of the online marketing tactics. Some of the optimizations that come with these platforms are unlimited bandwidth, unlimited domains, many different hosting partners like MSSQL and MySQL, more ram space can be purchased, and to even name the servers can be an option. Premium accounts are great for making the most out of the e-commerce platforms that are going to help market the inventory.

Chapter 15 Avoiding Common Dropshipping Mistakes

Once you've decided to start dropshipping, you need to ensure you have a solid business strategy in place, right from the start. This means you should be ready to avoid all these common mistakes. Let's take a look at these now.

Expecting Products to Sell

As previously mentioned, dropshipping (by design) places you in a competitive situation, for the reason that others are marketing precisely the same thing you are. It's all too laid-back an idea to contemplate that you'll be setting up drop shipping for your online store and that you will have an instant money-making scheme on your hands.

The exact opposite is true. With dropshipping, you need to place all of the time which you save on shipping and fulfillment into your marketing and SEO campaigns and efforts.

These are the elements which will drive customer traffic toward your store, and make you sales when you're a merchant who uses dropshipping. Since you can't control any side of the fulfillment or packaging/posting with dropshipping, you should always put a priority-focus on high-quality customer service. Additionally, you should make sure you give customers a positive and lasting experience in the areas of the purchasing process you find that you can control.

Reliant On One Supplier or Not Having a Backup Plan

If you only turn to one supplier without having any back-up, you're leaving yourself with logistical issues further down the line. What happens if your supplier raises prices to where you can't afford them? Or what if they go out of business? They might just decide to no longer work with you anymore, which can happen, too. I'm not big on "what ifs" in my personal life, but professionally I am, to stay ahead of the game.

Even on a less severe note, a supplier could be just out of stock on a product and be unable to answer when they'll have that stock in again, It's crucial to always have a backup supplier that you can turn to if your primary supplier doesn't work out for any particular reason/s.

Each time you start to work with a new supplier, you need to make sure that they perform, and you should place test orders to be sure. Once you get the order, examine it, and consider the packaging, the shipment time, and so on while making sure everything is the quality in which you expect. It is advisable to place test orders on a regular basis, although not detrimental. Fulfillment is as crucially important to any online business though, and you need to catch any dips in quality before they start becoming real issues.

Stressing Over Shipping Rates
Shipping rates can be an aggravation, even when you ship all your products from one location. If you ship from several warehouses or dropship via multiple suppliers, it can be a bit of a nightmare. What if an order draws on two different warehouses, or three different suppliers? Eeek!

Take a step back and take a good look at the bigger picture. What is it you aim to achieve? Is it better shipping rates? Or more sales and content customers who want repeat business? If you waste energy over shipping rates on every single order, that's energy not devoted to: creating better customer shopping experiences, increasing the size of your store, your marketing, and everything else you should focus on in terms of customer happiness, overall.

Take a look at previous orders, and use these to calculate flat shipping rates, or maybe tiered rates based on cart value. Will it slice into your profit margins? Yes, on some fulfilled orders. The difference is, you will come out ahead of others, and if you've set your rates correctly, shipping costs should be even cheaper, over time.

It has also been shown that flat prices and free shipping increases conversion rates. One primary reason that customers abandon their shopping carts is due to high shipping costs. Flat shipping fees remove confusion and superficially "hidden" fees which show up at checkout.

Chapter 16 Tips for Succeeding with Your Online Business

Mostly dropshipping products are sold on the basis of impulse buying. So there is a need to push the items right under the nose of the prospective buyers instead of just waiting for them to visit the dropshipping store.

Promoting the Products on Social Platforms

Social media is one amongst the most powerful means to promote, distribute content, advertise, and to acquire customers. For example, Facebook has more than one and a half billion users with varied backgrounds and lifestyles. So naturally, it is a very attractive platform for digital marketers to promote their products.

You can use these platforms for popularizing your product. But you should remember that content plays a vital role. Even if the platform is big and the product is great if it does not have an impressive content to back it, your efforts will be futile.

It has been tested and confirmed that people purchase drop shipping products from platforms like Facebook, Pinterest, and Instagram.

Influencer Marketing on Instagram

Nowadays, influencer marketing occupies an important place in the customer acquisition plans of online retailers. It is especially very effective for trendy niches. For example, if you want to sell a new type of handbag and you ask a popular figure on Instagram to include your handbag in one of her posts and tag your business, you are sure to win a big batch of new customers.

You can use Instagram influencers to promote your products. These are the people who have a large following on Instagram. They are of three types: celebrities, social influencers, and micro influencers.

- Celebrities: Movie actors, sportspersons, artists, politicians, and social workers belong to this category. They are powerful and generally do not work with small enterprises.

- Social influencers: They have more than ten thousand followers. They do not restrict themselves to one niche alone. They charge high rates for promotion work and usually work with more than one brand at a time.

- Micro influencers: They have five thousand to ten thousand followers. They are confined to a niche. They can be very helpful for promoting the products which belong to only one niche. They charge lower rates for promoting your posts.

If you choose to do influencer marketing pick one niche and select influencers who are more impressive, make sure that their post has a minimum of five hearts or comments.

Start pitching after you have noted down the names of 5 - 10 influencers. You can tell them that they may keep the item if they post its picture in their account on Instagram.

Google Ads and Facebook Ads

Google and Facebook advertising are different in nature. Google shows advertisements which are related to the keywords used for searching by the user. While Facebook

Ads function on the basis of user information. The interests of the users are noted which are called data points. It displays ads on the basis of these data points for the users.

Benefits of Google Ads

- You can gain good exposure in the search results.
- They give you a chance to advertise on the world's largest platforms like YouTube, and Google search.
- It is easy to target specific demographics like language, location, and device.
- You can use high volume key phrases or keywords which are related to the niche you are dealing with and maximize exposure.

Benefits of Facebook Ads

- They help you to start your business easily.
- You can control the amount of money you spend every day.
- It is possible for you to target specific demographics like location, and interests.
- You can get quick results.
- They are useful for increasing brand awareness.
- Good ads or boosted posts can become viral.

PPC Advertising

PPC advertising is allowed on many social media platforms. Facebook ads are an example of this. Another platform which is popular for advertising is Google AdWords.

Customer Reviews and Ratings

Customer reviews make a lot of difference in this type of enterprise. Just a few negative reviews can actually ruin the entire business. You can see how people buy products online from eBay and Amazon. The decision to purchase things on the basis of the rating of the product and the comments of the customers about it.

The same thing is applicable to your drop shipping store. A few good reviews can boost the reputation of your website and products. The best way of getting accolades from the customers is to cater to them in the best possible manner.

If you offer high-quality goods, a remarkable customer support service and quick delivery of items, you can surely make your mark and get good feedback from the customers.

This feedback can be utilized as a testimonial for the website and can help to acquire more customers.

Email Marketing

You can use email marketing to inform your clients about the changes in your company. You can inform them about the price changes, and the discounts offered. Emails may be used for conveying content related to the product or the industry.

Mail-Chimp can be very useful for this purpose. It automates some processes, creates and saves templates, and produces analytics and reports.

This type of marketing is more complex and is usually used for the purpose of remarketing. That means after collecting your buyers' emails, you can sell your new products to them by sending the information about the products through email. You can use automation software such as Campaign Monitor, Get-Response, Mail-Chimp, or A-Weber for this purpose.

Customer Support

An efficient customer support service can provide better customer satisfaction and thereby help to boost your business.

You can adopt any of these methods which are generally used by the e-commerce industry. They are:

- Phone support: Phone is a quick and efficient means of connecting with the client directly. It is easier to deal with tricky situations by phone. It also enables you to get quick feedback from your client. Google Voice can be useful for this purpose.

- Email support: You can use email for providing support to your customers. It is a good idea to create emails which bear the name of your domain, for example, hello@domainname.com. This will give it a professional look, and your brand will be impressive for the customers. You can use Help-scout which is a very suitable software for email support.

- Support through social media: Sometimes customers look at the pages of the brands on social media even before they contact a particular brand. The customers can find answers to their questions there as social media which is a forum for the public already has answers for them.

A good representative who provides customer support through social media can help to set up good relations between the brand and the customers.

- Live chat: Many brands incorporate the live chatting facility on the websites to provide customer support. This method has become very popular. It enables customers to get support quickly. It is less intimidating than posting questions on some public forum.

But if your business has not expanded much this type of support is not needed. This option may be suitable after you have scaled your business. Another option is to utilize the facility for direct messages on Twitter and Instagram or use Facebook Messenger.

Other Marketing Methods

There are some marketing strategies which are inexpensive or free of cost but have slow results. Some of them are:

Forum or Blog Marketing

You can look for forums or blogs which are associated with your niche or products and actively participate in the discussions. You can represent your particular niche and include your website's link. In this way, you may increase the traffic and get new customers to your online store.

Growth Hacking

This method is not expensive, and at the same time, it is highly effective to get creative campaigns for marketing online. Retargeting the old campaigns or appearing as guest bloggers for popular websites in your niches are some examples of growth hacking. Essentially it comprises of content marketing.

Content Marketing

This involves a process of creating valuable content to acquire an audience which can be converted into customers. It is not an explicit way of advertising. The content should be about serving the audience than about serving your brand. It can be in the form of a trendy Instagram post, a witty post on Twitter, or a blog.

Conclusion

Starting a dropshipping business is an incredible way to earn yourself a six-figure income. There are many ways to start a dropshipping business, but this streamlined guide will allow you to start one efficiently and reach your six-figure income as quickly as possible. Even though drop shipping is a passive income stream, you should be prepared to put in a fair amount of work to establish your business. Once you establish your business and have regular sales on your website, you can hire assistants and remove yourself from the business, making it an even more passive income source.

I hope that this book was able to clearly guide you through the process of starting your own drop- shipping business. Each chapter was designed to be a clear and concise guide walking you through each step of the business so that you can start with a strong plan. By following this guide, you will certainly be able to start your own business with the potential to earn you a six-figure income.

The next step is for you to start putting these plans into action. If you haven't been working step-by-step throughout the book, then it is time to go back to the beginning and start implementing the strategies to develop your drop shipping business. Make sure that you pay close attention to the common mistakes and tips and tricks that have been outlined in this book as they will provide you with the knowledge you need to strategize and have a strong start in your drop shipping business. That way, you can ensure that you set yourself up for total success.

Thank you, and I wish you the best of luck in creating your six-figure dropshipping business.

www.ingramcontent.com/pod-product-compliance
Lightning Source LLC
Chambersburg PA
CBHW072023230526
45466CB00019B/72